CHARISMATIC RELIGION
IN MODERN RESEARCH:
A BIBLIOGRAPHY

For Michael

CHARISMATIC RELIGION IN MODERN RESEARCH: A BIBLIOGRAPHY

NABPR Bibliographic Series, Number 1

by
Watson E. Mills

 MERCER UNIVERSITY PRESS, Macon, Georgia 31207

ISBN 0-86554-143-4

All books published by Mercer University Press are produced
on acid-free paper that exceeds the minimum standards set by the
National Historical Publications and Records Commission.

TABLE OF CONTENTS

EDITOR'S NOTE:

Watson E. Mills, professor of Religion and Vice President for Research and Publication at Mercer University, has agreed to launch the National Association for Baptist Professors of Religion *Bibliographic Series* with the publication of *Charismatic Religion in Modern Research: A Bibliography*. Other contributions to this series are invited. Bibliographies may range from 75 to 200 pages. They may reflect the standardized form illustrated in the Mills bibliography, or they may be composed in essay form. Should you have a bibliography that you wish to propose for this series, send your proposal to Dr. David M. Scholer, Northern Baptist Theological Seminary, 660 East Butterfield Road, Lombard, Illinois, 60148.

PREFACE

The incentive for the examination of charismatic religion grows out of the persistent conviction that—however legitimate its solutions—its existence serves to underscore a real problem within Christendom today, namely, there exist less than adequate categories for dealing with the experience of the Spirit.

Charismatic religion, at root, is a protest against an institutional church that is excessively bureaucratic and increasingly over-gorged with nominal members. Charismatics expect, if not demand, that the Holy Spirit be as real a part of the faith today as it has been in the past.

The church is a long way from that point! Much study, discussion and debate will occur before any consensus could emerge. This bibliography is offered as a tool to that worthy end.

I wish to thank Ms. Irene Pace who worked tirelessly in the typing of each of the drafts of this manuscript. She also assisted in verifying the publication data. She was ably assisted by Ms. Sandra Keaton. To these I express deep appreciation.

Watson E. Mills
Macon, Georgia
August 1984

INTRODUCTION

If the charismatic movement is the "Cinderella of theology,"[1] then attempting to catalogue the diverse and expansive literature it has produced may also require the services of a fairy godmother. Indeed, with the publication (and subsequent English translation) of Walter Hollenweger's *Enthusiastisches Christentum: Die Pfingstbewegung in Geschichte und Gegenwart*[2] in 1966, world Pentecostalism was meticulously catalogued and thrust upon an unprepared and unsuspecting Christendom. Today, no one would doubt the size and importance of this new force. Gradually, the vocabulary of Christendom has come to include the term *charisma* which refers generally to a zest and an enthusiasm for the faith that was not usually found, at least heretofore, among the more staid denominational forms of the faith.

The sheer numbers of those caught up in charismatic religion pointed to a reality with which Christendom would have to reckon. Once convenient stereotypes were rendered sterile. Charismatic religion began to move from the closet to the mainstream of Christendom.

Though it is too early to be certain, this "new" force in the Christian world, born of this century out of the dispossessed of American society, may well be the major contribution of this nation to world Christianity in the twentieth century. Indeed, today the charismatic type of religion is the fastest growing major form of Christianity in the third world nations.

In the aftermath of Hollenweger's epoch making work, the production of literature relating to charismatic religion increased at an unbelievable rate. The

---

[1]G. J. Sirks, "The Cinderella of Theology: The Doctrine of the Holy Spirit," *Harvard Theological Review*, 50 (April 1957): 77.

[2]Walter Hollenweger's multi-volume dissertation written at the University of Zurich and entitled "Handbuch der Pfingstbewegung," in all of its enormity, is a gold mine of historical and statistical information on world Pentecostalism. Happily for the layman, Hollenweger summarized that work into a German publication (1966) entitled "Enthusiastisches Christentum Die Pfingstwewegung in Geschichte und Gegenwart" published by Rolf Brockhaus. In 1972 this epoch making work appeared from the Augsburg Publishing House under the English title *The Pentecostals: The Charismatic Movement in the Churches*. The work contains a 35 page annotated bibliography.

attempt is made here to identify and catalogue these materials into a single bibliography that will provide the broadest possible acquaintance with this enormous body of literature. Certainly, in the strictest sense, this effort will necessarily fail. The sources are too diverse for any single researcher, or team of researchers, to assemble successfully a definitive list. That fact notwithstanding, I have set out to amass a bibliography that will give attention to charismatic religion in its classic form (Pentecostalism), in its more recent form (neo-Pentecostalism), and in its non-denominational form (the Jesus movement). Thus this bibliography includes works that are oriented toward classic Pentecostalism as well as more recent works that treat the "penetration" of classic Pentecostalism into the mainline denominations, a phenomenon often referred to as neo-Pentecostalism. Of course, this aspect of the movement widened its scope enormously and created a base from which much literature would arise. Millions of Christians are involved in this sweep of the mainline churches including Catholicism. Another evidence of the extent of the presence of charismatic religion in Christendom, particularly in the late 60s and 70s is the Jesus movement. Unlike neo-Pentecostalism this particular expression developed *outside* the confines of the institutional church.

But with all of its expressions, charismatic religion focuses upon the genuine and "real" role of the Holy Spirit in the lives of is adherents. Often, though not always, this "presence" of the Spirit is attested to by the presence of the gifts of the Spirit, notably, but not necessarily, glossolalia or "speaking in tongues."

DEFINITIONS

In writing a bibliographic essay and assembling a major bibliography, some stipulative definitions were necessary. In this work, the term "charismatic"[3] is used to refer to anyone, regardless of denominational preference, if any, if that person

> places emphasis upon the role of the Spirit in his/her life *and* seeks to demonstrate its presence through the attainment of the Baptism of the Holy Spirit

---

[3]Some writers insist on distinguishing between the term "charismatic" (one who has received the Pentecostal blessing but who retains existing denominational affiliation) and "Pentecostal." Initially in the early 60s there was no single term to refer to mainliners who received the baptism of the Holy Spirit. The term neo-Pentecostal evolved slowly in the late 60s. A pejorative way of referring to growing numbers of new charismatics was the use of the term "tongues movement" which, of course, is phenomenological rather than theological. In this volume, I will use the term charismatic in the broadest sense. For a fuller discussion see Peter Hocken, "The Pentecostal-Charismatic Movement as Revival and Renewal," *Pneuma*, 3:1 (1981): 31-47.

as evidenced by the presence of spiritual gifts which include, among others, "speaking in tongues."

Such a definition would then include Christians who may then be described as: 1) Pentecostal, that is one who belongs to any of the traditional Pentecostal denominations; 2) neo-Pentecostal, that is one who belongs to any of the traditional non-Pentecostal denominations, including the Roman Catholic church; and 3) nondenominational, that is one who is not aligned to any Pentecostal or non-Pentecostal group.

EXCLUSIONS

This bibliography includes only a random sampling of "testimonia"—of which there are literally thousands. Similarly, a few examples of the largely uninformed denunciations of charismatic religion that grew up in the 60s and early 70s are included for the sake of illustration—most are omitted.

By the very nature of the subject being addressed, there are a large number of privately published works that are cited in this bibliography even when full documentation regarding publisher and date were unavailable.

Works that deal with charismatic religion outside the United States are generally excluded except where these afford specific insight into its importance and development in this country.

EXTANT BIBLIOGRAPHIES

While there is no extant bibliography that accomplishes what has been set as the goal here, there are certain bibliographies that may be used in conjunction with this one to extend its usefulness into areas that have been excluded from its scope.

While it contains no bibliographic essay as such, the two volume work by Charles Jones entitled *A Guide to the Study of Pentecostal Movement*[4] (2 vols. American Theological Library Association/Scarecrow Press, 1983) is useful because it details much of the literature that reflects Pentecostal self-assessment. Another important feature is the detailed organization of the material. There are helpful tables, appendices, extensive biographies of Pentecostal/neo-Pentecostal writers and a comprehensive index.

An older, far briefer, but insightful essay is that by David W. Faupel. His *The American Pentecostal Movement: A Bibliographic Essay* was published in

---

[4]Also helpful is Charles Edwin Jones, *A Guide to the Study of the Holiness Movement* (American Theological Library Association/Scarecrow Press, 1974).

1972 by the Asbury Theological Library as monograph number one of the newly created Society for Pentecostal Studies.

There are two bibliographies on the Jesus movement worthy of mention: a short one by Erling Jorstad entitled "A Review Essay of Sources and Interpretations of the Jesus Movement," appeared in the *Lutheran Quarterly*.[5] A longer and more complete bibliography is "Jesus Movement," Center of Research and Documentation of Christian Institutes, #4, published by Bibliographical Catalogue of Christian Institutions (CERDIC), Université des Sciences Humaines de Strasbourg, 1973.

There are several bibliographies available on glossolalia. Among these are Ira J. Martin, *The Gift of Tongues: A Bibliography* (Pathway Press, 1970) and Watson E. Mills, *Speaking in Tongues: A Classified Bibliography* (Society for Pentecostal Studies, 1974).

SURVEYS OF CHARISMATIC RELIGION

There are many volumes that could be read with profit on this subject. Three will be suggested. The first is an anthology edited by Canon Michael P. Hamilton, "The Charismatic Movement," (Eerdmans, 1975). The volume offers an interdisciplinary analysis of the strengths and weaknesses of charismatic religion. It is a highly readable work consisting of four major sections with ten essays. The contributors come from both charismatic and non-charismatic traditions. In addition to bibliographies at the end of each chapter, there is a general bibliography at the conclusion of the volume together with a short phonograph record that contains a sample of tongue speech. Also of significance is *Gifts of the Spirit in the Body of Christ: Perspectives on the Charismatic Movement*, edited by J. Elmo Agrimson (Augsburg Publishing House, 1974). The six essays in this anthology deal with a range of spiritual gifts and the ways these relate to the body of Christ. A Pentecostal writer, Vinson Synan has edited a volume entitled *Aspects of Pentecostal-Charismatic Origins* (Logos International, 1975). The volume contains eleven essays, largely written by charismatic participants (one notable exception being Marty's article entitled "Pentecostalism in the Context of American Piety and Practice").

Certainly any discussion of the impact of charismatic religion on the world scene will require an examination of Hollenweger's works (already cited above). In addition, a standard Pentecostal treatment of the subject is John Thomas Nichol, *Pentecostalism* (Harper and Row, 1966). Growing out of

---

[5]Erling Jorstad, "A Review Essay of Sources and Interpretations of the Jesus Movement," *The Lutheran Quarterly*, 25 (1973): 295-303.

a doctoral dissertation done at Boston University, this excellent work documents the rise of Pentecostal movements internationally in relation to the origin of Pentecostalism in America.

CHARISMATIC RELIGION IN AMERICAN DENOMINATIONALISM

David J. DuPlessis, a former Assemblies of God minister from South Africa, is generally credited for having introduced the Pentecostal experience into the mainline denominations. An active participant in the Second Vatican Council, and longtime executive secretary for the World Pentecostal Conference, DuPlessis had regular contact with denominational officials from many other denominational groups including Roman Catholics. His autobiographical account of his work in this area is entitled *The Spirit Bade Me Go: The Astounding Move of God in the Denominational Churches* (published by the author, 1960). The book is a popular treatment and has undergone several revisions.

In tracing the development of neo-Pentecostalism,[6] most historians look to a Sunday morning in April 1960 when Pastor Dennis J. Bennett, then minister of the Van Nuys Episcopal Church, confessed to his congregation that he had been secretly involved in the charismatic revival. Bennett later wrote a work entitled *Nine O'Clock in the Morning* (Logos International, 1970) which details the account of his involvement with charismatic religion including speaking in tongues. In 1971, he teamed with his wife to write *The Holy Spirit and You* (Logos International, 1971). This latter work has proved helpful to those from other theological traditions who have become interested in the Pentecostal experience. Another popular work is that by John L. Sherrill, *They Speak with Other Tongues* (McGraw Hill, 1964). Sherrill, a newspaper reporter, set out to document the Pentecostal/charismatic experience. To his surprise, he himself became caught up in the movement and the resulting book describes his personal pilgrimage.

Theological guidelines for a charismatic congregation seeking renewal within the framework of the institutional church are set forth in Heribert Mühlen, *A Charismatic Theology* (Paulist Press, 1978).

---

[6]A single source for documents relating to charismatic renewal is Kilian McDonnell, editor, *Presence, Power, Praise: Documents on the Charismatic Renewal* (3 vols.; Liturgical Press, 1980). Volumes 1 and 2 contain 80 documents dated between 1960 and 1979 that are continental, national, and regional in scope while the 11 documents in volume 3 are international.

CLASSIFICATION OF CHARISMATIC GROUPS[7]

The term charismatic is an inclusive term often applied to a large number of sects, assemblies and churches. Many have risen out of a Methodist or Baptist background, though not all. Some of the largest groups, and sample sub-groupings, will be mentioned here.

1. Pentecostal Groups

The largest single identifiable segment within charismatic religion today is the various Pentecostal groups that came into being largely in the United States in this century. Until about 1920 the Pentecostal movement had no standard doctrine because of the pluralism represented in its membership. Most adherents, however, were primarily concerned with perfectionism, holiness and the baptism of the Holy Spirit.

These groups are the most prevalent in the south, midwest, and west. There is great variety in the names employed and the term "Pentecostal" does *not* necessarily occur in each. The *Handbook of Denominations in the U.S.* lists the following subgroups of Pentecostals:

Calvary Pentecostal Church, Inc.
Elim Missionary Assemblies
Pentecostal Fire-Baptized Holiness Church
Pentecostal Holiness Church
International Pentecostal Assemblies
Pentecostal Assemblies of the World, Inc.
Pentecostal Church of Christ
Pentecostal Church of God of America, Inc.
United Pentecostal Church, Inc.

The paucity of this list becomes apparent when compared with that produced by Charles Edwin Jones in *A Guide to the Study of the Pentecostal*

---

[7]The most definitive classification of charismatic religion, among its Pentecostal representatives is that offered by Charles Edwin Jones, *A Guide to the Study of the Pentecostal Movement* (2 vols.; American Theological Library Association/Scarecrow Press, 1983). Klaude Kendrick, *The Promise Fulfilled: A History of the Modern Pentecostal Movement* (Gospel Publishing House, 1961) was the first scholar to group Pentecostal bodies by issues that were determinative in their being formed into separate denominations.

Movement. Jones lists more than 400 different groups and divides them into the following categories:[8]

> Wesleyan-Arminian Tradition
> 1. Holiness—Pentecostal Bodies
> 2. Signs—Following Bodies
> Finished Work of Calvary or Baptistic Tradition
> 1. Trinitarian Bodies
> 2. Oneness Bodies

Jones' classification of the various groups along doctrinal lines is the enlargement and refinement of a system first introduced in 1954 by Everett L. Moore.[9] Moore identified three categories of Pentecostals: 1) those who hold a Keswick view of sanctification; 2) those who hold a Holiness view of "entire" sanctification; 3) those who hold a "Jesus only" view of the God-head.

In 1971, Pentecostal scholarship took a bold new direction with the publication of Vinson Synan's *The Holiness Pentecostal Movement in the United States* (Eerdmans, 1971). Synan analyzes Pentecostalism as a direct descendant of the Holiness movement which itself can be traced through Methodism and Anglicanism, to the Roman Catholic church. Synan's thesis is that Pentecostalism arose *outside* of reformed theology. One of the ways he supports his contention is to show how key leaders in the early days of the movement came out of the holiness tradition. Charles Fox Parham,[10] for example, was the first modern-day theologian to equate glossolalia with the baptism of the Holy Spirit.[11] Parham, notes Synan, was a Methodist lay minister. It is through his student, William J. Seymour, that Synan traces Parham's influence to the famous Azusa Street mission.[12]

Azusa Street was not only the spark that ignited the Pentecostal revival, but in its earliest days, most of the doctrinal issues surfaced there that would

---

[8]Charles Edwin Jones, *A Guide to the Study of the Pentecostal Movement* (2 vols.; American Theological Library Association/Scarecrow Press, 1983), pp. xi-xxii. Jones' listing gives credence to the 1966 claim of Walter Hollenweger who boasted knowledge of at least 200 Pentecostal groups. Hollenweger, *op. cit.*, p. 19.

[9]Everett L. Moore, "Handbook of Pentecostal Denominations." Unpublished master's thesis, Pasadena College, 1954.

[10]For a biography, see Sarah E. Parham, *The Life of Charles F. Parham: Founder of the Apostolic Faith Movement*, Tri-State Printing Company, 1930.

[11]An intriguing autobiography of the first person to speak in tongues under Parham's ministry is Agnes Ozman LaBerge, *What God Hath Wrought*, Herald Publishing Company, 1921.

[12]The centrality of the Azusa Street mission to the understanding of the rise of Pentecostalism in the twentieth century is not disputed regardless of the credibility of Synan's thesis. Frank Bartleman's *How Pentecost Came to Los Angeles* (privately published, 1925) is a first-hand account.

later become determinative for the formation of the major Pentecostal groups. Those issues were: 1) doctrine of sanctification; 2) Jesus-only doctrine; 3) latter rain covenant; and 4) race as a basis for denominational division.

Two years later Synan completed a study of the history of the Pentecostal Holiness church.[13] The church was organized in 1898 at Anderson, South Carolina. Building upon his earlier thesis, Synan successfully demonstrates the close ties of his denomination to Methodism. The most famous personality to emerge from the Pentecostal Holiness church is Oral Roberts.[14] The Pentecostal Holiness church taught three distinctive experiences: justification by grace; sanctification as a second work of faith; and Spirit baptism. The latter was attested to by the charismatic experience of glossolalia or "speaking in tongues." Services were regularly characterized as "joyous demonstrations" of the presence of God's spirit.

Another of the largest and oldest of the Pentecostal Holiness groups that places emphasis upon charismatic expression is the Church of God (Cleveland, Tennessee). Its origins can be traced by a conference held at Barney Creek meeting house in Monroe County, Tennessee, in 1886, though the name "Church of God" was not applied to this group until 1907. Under the leadership of A. J. Tomlinson the church became identified with the holiness movement. Charismatic elements in the Church of God include speaking in tongues, healing, and baptism of the Holy Spirit.[15]

There are countless other Pentecostal groups—all of which demonstrate an avid interest in the charismatic dimension of the faith.[16]

2. Neo-Pentecostal Groups

The "new" charismatics, as they are sometimes called, began to appear in the 50s as the older, classical Pentecostals began to share their charismatic experiences with non-Pentecostal Christians.

---

[13]See Vinson Synan, *The Old-Time Religion: A History of the Pentecostal Holiness Church*, Advocate Press, 1973. An older standard history is Joseph E. Campbell, *The Pentecostal Holiness Church 1898-1948: Its History and Background*, Publishing House of the Pentecostal Holiness Church, 1951.

[14]See Oral Roberts, *The Call*, Doubleday and Company, 1972, to see why he returned to the Methodist Church.

[15]Two denominational histories document the origin and growth of the Church of God. See E. L. Simmons, *History of the Church of God* (Church of God Publishing House, 1938) and Charles W. Conn, *Like a Mighty Army Moves the Church of God 1886-1955* (Church of God Publishing House, 1955).

[16]See Charles E. Jones, *A Guide to the Study of the Pentecostal Movement, op. cit.*, and Jones, *A Guide to the Study of the Holiness Movement, op. cit.*

By the early 50s, there was a growing disenchantment in the ranks of old-line Pentecostalism. Generally, there was dissatisfaction with what was perceived as limited vision and autocratic leadership. As the body of the disenchanted grew and gained financial backing, permanent support was forthcoming to inaugurate new programs and enlist new support. The rapid growth of the Full Gospel Business Men's Fellowship International clearly indicated the potential for charismatic religion *outside* the traditional Pentecostal circles. Founded by Demos Shakarian, a successful California dairyman reared in a Pentecostal home, the FGBMFI grew naturally out of the post-war mass revivals that unified Pentecostals all over the world.[17]

In 1951 Shakarian helped to organize the Oral Roberts Los Angeles campaign. Out of this meeting came the FGBMFI. Initially, the call went out for Pentecostals who wanted the "full experience" of the Christian life but who were being held back under the burdensome restrictions of oldline Pentecostalism. Quickly, this new alliance of charismatic businessmen spread across the U.S. and around the world. From its beginning the organization reached a new type of audience in settings far removed from the camp meetings of the oldline Pentecostal denominations. Meetings of local chapters, often staged in plush hotels, displayed the traditional charismatic vigor but in radically new surroundings. A broader and much more sophisticated audience became aware of the charismatic dimension of the faith. A figure of no less prominence than Walter Hollenweger concluded that the FGBMFI can claim credit for having gained a hearing for the healing evangelists in the non-Pentecostal churches.[18] The FGBMFI was responsible for introducing charismatic religion to hundreds of thousands of middle-class Americans.

Some of the strategies in the practice of charismatic religion had to be revised, others discarded. A new breed of people were the targets for its ministry.[19]

Oral Roberts, a keen observer of the changing mix in the makeup of the charismatics, moved slowly but resolutely in the 60s to insure that no innovation escaped his close scrutiny. In 1967, for instance, he abandoned his televised healing crusades after 13 successful years. In 1968 he joined the prestigious Boston Avenue Methodist Church in Tulsa—a decision which

---

[17]"The Story of Demos Shakarian and the Full Gospel Business Men's Fellowship," *The Voice of Deliverance* (August 1953): 9.

[18]Hollenweger, *op. cit.*, p. 6.

[19]Oral Roberts established the first important magazine published by an independent charismatic ministry. His magazine went through a series of name changes: *Healing Waters* (November 1947-August 1953), *America's Healing Magazine* (September 1953-December 1955), *Healing* (January 1956-July 1956), and *Abundant Life* (July 1956-). Roberts' magazine had a number of able editors, but the evangelist himself exercised close control over its contents.

shocked Pentecostal observers. The dedication of Oral Roberts University in 1967 marked the unique blending of charismatic religion and higher education—in an accredited university!

Perhaps more than any other figure,[20] Oral Roberts, with a newly designed TV series airing in prime time slots in all major U.S. markets, and a going university, has put the face of respectability upon the practice of charismatic religion.[21]

On another front, earlier on in the 60s, neo-Pentecostalism was recognized as a respectable component of ecumenical Christianity. In April 1960, then rector of St. Mark's Episcopal Church in Van Nuys, California, Reverend Dennis Bennett, confessed to his congregation his own personal involvement for some months with charismatic religion in general, and speaking in tongues in particular.[22] Bennett had been reared a Congregationalist but had been converted to the Episcopal church in 1951 upon completion of his theological studies at Chicago Divinity School. He vowed not to leave the Episcopal ministry even though he was asked to leave St. Mark's. By July of 1960 he was called to be the rector of St. Luke's Episcopal Church in Seattle, a church of about 200 apathetic members. Within the course of one year 80 of those members had received the baptism of the Holy Spirit. By 1968 there were more than 2,000 members at St. Luke's and Dennis Bennett was now cropping up in every major denomination. Michael Harper has written the best account tracing the development of the charismatic revival among the mainline denominations: *As At the Beginning: The Twentieth Century Pentecostal Revival* (Hodder & Stoughton, 1965). As early as 1963 the spread of charismatic religion into the mainline churches received national attention in an article by Frank Farrell entitled "Outburst of Tongues: The New Penetration," *Christianity Today*, 7 (September 13, 1963): 3-7. The relationship of old-time Pentecostalism to charismatic experiences among non-Pentecostal denominations

---

[20]Many Pentecostal scholars cite the work of David J. DuPlessis as central in introducing Pentecostalism into the mainline denominations. As a longtime executive secretary for the World Pentecostal Conference, DuPlessis was in a unique position to contact leaders in the World Council of Churches. His autobiographical *The Spirit Bade Me Go: The Astounding Move of God in the Denominational Churches* (Logos International, 1972) is still available and documents this fascinating story.

[21]In more recent years, the liberal religious press has come to show a much greater respect for the charismatic movement. A few examples might include: Allen Walker, "Where Pentecostalism is Mushrooming," *Christian Century* 85 (January 17, 1968): 81-82; "The Gift of Tongues," *Christianity Today* (April 11, 1969), 27-28; Jeffery L. Klaiber, "Pentecostal Breakthrough," *America* 122 (January 31, 1970): 99-102.

[22]See Dennis J. Bennett, *Nine O'Clock in the Morning* (Logos International, 1970). See also Dennis and Rita Bennett, *The Holy Spirit and You* (Logos International, 1971).

is the subject of a paper by Peter Hocken entitled "The Pentecostal-Charismatic Movement as Revival and Renewal," *Pneuma*, 3:1 (Spring 1981): 31-47.

The "new penetration" of charismatic religion into mainline churches was marked by the involvement of lay leaders. One early example is Jean Stone who was a member of Dennis Bennett's congregation at Van Nuys. She was an affluent housewife who organized The Blessed Trinity Society in 1961 after being baptized by the Spirit at a prayer meeting in 1960 at St. Mark's. The Society was aimed at emphasizing the work of the third member of the trinity. The Society published a magazine called *Trinity*. Gradually, the seminars sponsored by The Blessed Trinity Society came to be known as "charismatic clinics" because invariably they featured charismatic testimonies and speaking in tongues. In 1966 Stone divorced and remarried on her way to Hong Kong to serve as a "faith missionary" in the charismatic movement there. The Blessed Trinity Society was absorbed into Melodyland, an organization then headed by David Wilkerson. *Trinity* became the *Logos Journal* and the *New Covenant* which remain the leading periodicals of the charismatic movement today.[23]

The Catholic charismatic movement[24] is usually traced to the involvement of lay faculty members at Duquesne University in Pittsburgh in February of 1967. The so-called "Duquesne Weekend" saw about 30 people receive the gift of the Holy Spirit. From Duquesne, Catholic interest in charismatic religion quickly spread to Notre Dame and to Michigan State University. The resulting campus charismatic groups began to meet with local chapters of the FGBMFI, and by the summer of 1967 more than 3,000 Catholic charismatics attended "Notre Dame Weekend." To the chagrin of church leaders, most were priests, nuns, or teaching monks.

Several books on charismatic religion among Catholics are worthy of note. One of the first to appear was that by Kevin and Dorothy Ranaghan, *Catholic Pentecostals* (Paulist-Neuman Press, 1969). It is an excellent historical account of the development of the Catholic charismatic religion. Also significant

---

[23]Some of the additional, more prominent, charismatic periodicals include: *Charisma Digest*, Full Gospel Business Men's Fellowship International; *Cross and Switchblade*, Teen Challenge Publications; *Heartbeat*, Charismatic Educational Centers, Inc.; *New Nation News*, Texas Soul Clinic; *New Wine*, Holy Spirit Teaching Missions; *Voice*, Full Gospel Business Men's Fellowship International.

[24]For an excellent definitive bibliography on Catholic Pentecostalism see Edward D. O'Connor, editor, *Perspectives on Charismatic Renewal* (University of Notre Dame Press, 1975), pp. 156-84. Earlier, shorter bibliographies include: John Gordon Melton, *Catholic Pentecostal Movement: A Bibliography* (Institute for the Study of American Religion, 1976); Edward D. O'Connor, *The Pentecostal Movement in the Catholic Church* (Ave Maria Press, 1971), pp. 295-301; Peter Hocken, "Pentecostals on Paper," *The Clergy Review*, 59:11 (November 1974): 750-67; 60:3 (March 1975): 161-83; 60:6 (June 1975): 344-67.

is Kilian McDonnell, *Charismatic Renewal and the Churches* (The Seabury Press, 1976). He offers a sociological analysis of the movement by summarizing the official responses to the charismatic movement by American denominations.[25] Another important Catholic charismatic writer is Edward D. O'Connor. His *The Pentecostal Movement in the Catholic Church* (Ave Maria Press, 1971) and his *Perspectives on Charismatic Renewal* (University of Notre Dame Press, 1975) are especially helpful.

Donald L. Gelpi and J. Massyngberde Ford offer helpful insights into the significance of charismatic religion for the church. See especially Donald L. Gelpi, *Experiencing God: A Theology of Human Experience* (Paulist Press, 1978) and his earlier *Pentecostalism: A Theological Viewpoint* (Paulist Press, 1971). Gelpi also contributed an insightful chapter entitled "Pentecostal Theology: A Roman Catholic Viewpoint," in *Perspectives on the New Pentecostalism*, Russell F. Spittler, editor (Baker Book House, 1976), pp. 86-103. J. Massyngberde Ford has contributed widely to the discussion of Catholic Pentecostalism. Among her more notable works are: *The Pentecostal Experience: A New Direction for American Catholics* (Paulist Press, 1970); "The Catholic Charismatic Gifts in Worship," in *The Charismatic Movement*, Michael Hamilton, editor (Eerdmans, 1975), pp. 114-23; *Baptism of the Spirit: Three Essays on the Pentecostal Experience* (Divine Word Publications, 1971).

Kilian McDonnell, executive director of the Institute for Ecumenical and Cultural Research, Collegeville, Minnesota, has taken the lead in addressing the question of the ecumenical significance of the charismatic movement. See his *The Charismatic Renewal and Ecumenism* (Paulist Press, 1978) and "Towards a Critique of the Churches and the Charismatic Renewal," *One in Christ*, 16:4 (1980): 329-37. See also Kilian McDonnell and Arnold Bittlinger, *The Baptism in the Holy Spirit as an Ecumenical Problem* (Charismatic Renewal Services, 1972). A good view of the present status of charismatic Catholic religion is a statement drafted by Kilian McDonnell for a conference of churchmen held in Milines, Belgium, May 1974: *Theological and Pastoral Orientations on Catholic Charismatic Renewal* (The World of Life, 1974).

3. The Jesus Movement

Like the rise of classic Pentecostalism in the twentieth century, the Jesus movement of the late sixties and early seventies stands outside the mainstream of organized, institutional Christianity. There are two excellent introductions

---

[25]See *Presence, Power, Praise: Documents of the Charismatic Renewal* (3 vols.; Liturgical Press, 1980). This represents the definitive collection of such papers and documents, national and international in scope.

to the movement: Ronald M. Enroth, et al., *The Jesus People* (Eerdmans Publishing, 1972) and Robert S. Ellwood, Jr., *One Way: The Jesus Movement and Its Meaning* (Prentice-Hall, 1973). An attempt to evaluate the significance of the movement from the vantage point of evangelical theology is William S. Cannon, *The Jesus Revolution* (Broadman Press, 1971).

Primary sources include autobiographical works by leaders of the movement. See Duane Pederson, *Jesus People* (Compass Press, 1972). Pederson gives his personal account of how he came to the Jesus movement and how he later founded the *Hollywood Free Paper*. The book is aimed at showing the centrality of charismatic expression in the Jesus movement. Also, Arthur Blessitt, *Turned on to Jesus* (Hawthorne Books, 1971) and Donald M. Williams, *Call to the Streets* (Augsburg Publishing House, 1972).

GLOSSOLALIA

Certainly there is no more controversial aspect of charismatic religion than speaking in tongues. A good general survey of the phenomenon remains that of George B. Cutten, *Speaking with Tongues: Historically and Psychologically Considered* (Yale University Press, 1927). A brief introduction is Frank Stagg, et al., *Glossolalia: Tongue-Speaking in Biblical, Historical, and Psychological Perspective* (Abingdon Press, 1967). Three professors from Southern Baptist Theological Seminary teamed together to write an introduction to the phenomenon of tongues. The treatment is sympathetic but it is the product of three persons who are not directly involved in charismatic religion. The best overview from the charismatic perspective is that of Wade Horton, editor, *The Glossolalia Phenomenon* (Pathway Press, 1966). This compilation of articles by prominent persons in the charismatic movement, treats the subject from historical and theological aspects as well.

One of the earliest studies of the movement, if not the most definitive to date, is Lincoln M. Vivier's unpublished dissertation entitled simply "Glossolalia," (Johannesburg, South Africa: University of Witwatersrand, 1960). This exhaustive work treats the biblical evidence and traces the historical occurrences of tongues between the first century and the twentieth. It contains a number of case studies which the author evaluates for psychological "hints." The resultant charismatic profile is one in which charismatic participants are slightly above average in psychological adjustment. While this conclusion met with much skepticism in the 60s, further research in the 70s has supported Vivier's position. See James T. Richardson's "Psychological Interpretations of Glossolalia: A Reexamination of Research," *Journal for the Scientific Study of Religion*, 12 (1973): 199-207. Richardson reviews a series of studies about glossolalia and psychological maladjustment. On the basis of the studies examined, he concludes there is no relationship between psychological maladies and glossolalia—a contention already reached by Vivier a decade earlier.

Certainly the epoch making work in the psychological dimension of charismatic religion is that by John Kildahl, *The Psychology of Speaking in Tongues* (Harper and Row, 1972). Kildahl focuses on the personal experiences of individuals and suggests that tongue speaking should be understood as a variety of aberrant behavior, like neurosis and other psychogenic disorders. Kildahl used psychiatric interviews and batteries of psychological tests to document his conclusion that glossolalists were more submissive, suggestible, and dependent on leaders than were non-glossolalists. Glossolalists were found to initiate their speech in the presence of or by thinking and feeling emotionally "close" to some authority figure, either real or imagined.

THEOLOGICAL STUDIES

One of the classic examples of the theology of charismatic religion is Frederick Dale Bruner, *A Theology of the Holy Spirit: The Pentecostal Experience and the New Testament Witness* (Eerdmans, 1970) and James D. G. Dunn, *Baptism in the Holy Spirit: A Reexamination of the New Testament Teaching of the Gift of the Spirit in Relation to Pentecostalism Today* (SCM Press, 1970). Though neither of these writers stands within the Pentecostal tradition, both are successful in presenting the Pentecostal "distinctives." Bruner divides his work into two sections, dealing first with the Pentecostal understanding of the doctrine of the Spirit as it has developed historically and then finally moving to consider the biblical evidence for that understanding. Bruner's volume includes helpful appendices of important documents which have been utilized to extract the notion of the Pentecostal doctrine of the Spirit. He also provides a short, informative bibliographical essay on existing works together with an extensive bibliography. Dunn's work is not nearly so comprehensive as Bruner's, but is a careful, largely exegetical, study of the relevant portions of scripture.

Anthony Hoekema, *Holy Spirit Baptism* (Eerdmans, 1972) offers a thorough-going diatribe, based upon his understanding of scripture, *against* the major components of Pentecostal theology. His primary criticism is a fundamental one aimed at the basic presupposition of Pentecostal theology: Hoekema assails the teaching of a second blessing and offers the scriptural evidence that when a person is *first* baptized, the Holy Spirit already dwells within.

A conciliatory article entitled "The Significance of Glossolalia for the Church," appeared in *Speaking in Tongues: Let's Talk about It*, edited by Watson E. Mills (Word, 1973), pp. 143-51. In it, Wayne E. Ward seeks common ground for Pentecostals and non-Pentecostals alike. He finds the basis for this commonality within the local spiritual community, where all gifts are finally measured by their capacity for building up the body of the church.

A theology of Pentecostalism has never been written by a member of that tradition.[26] Early Pentecostal thinkers drew heavily on the work done by prominent Holiness theologians in the late nineteenth and early twentieth centuries.[27] Probably the most often quoted apologetic for Pentecostal theological distinctives is Carl Brumback, *What Meaneth This? A Pentecostal Answer to a Pentecostal Question* (Gospel Publishing House, 1947). One of the best known Pentecostal theologians in the world is Donald Gee, and Englishman who is noted for his many writings. among them are: *The Ministry Gifts of Christ* (Gospel Publishing House, 1930); *Concerning Spiritual Gifts* (Gospel Publishing House, 1947); and *Spiritual Gifts in the Work of the Ministry Today* (Gospel Publishing House, 1963).

---

[26]A Pentecostal Theology has never actually been written. Three early attempts, Myer Pearlman, *Knowing the Doctrines of the Bible* (Gospel Publishing House, 1937), Ernest S. Williams, *Systematic Theology*, (3 vols.; Gospel Publishing House, 1953), and P. C. Nelson, *Bible Doctrines: A Handbook on Pentecostal Theology* (South Western Press, 1936) were based largely on existing non-Pentecostal works and were designed to provide a basic structure in theology for a large number of clergy who had not had the opportunity of formal training.

[27]Representative titles of this era include R. A. Torrey, *The Holy Spirit* (Revell, 1927), Andrew Murray, *The Full Blessing of Pentecost* (Revell, 1908), A. J. Gordon, *The Ministry of the Spirit* (Revell, 1894), and Charles G. Finney, *Power from on High* (Victory Press, 1944). For further bibliography see Jones, *A Guide to Study of Holiness Movement*.

A

001 Abell, Troy D. *Better Felt Than Said: The Holiness Pentecostal Movement.* Markham Press, 1982.

002 Aberle, David. "A Note on Relative Deprivation Theory as Applied to Millenarian and Other Cultic Movements," in *Reader in Comparative Religion*, William A. Lessa and Evon Z. Vogt, editors. 2nd ed. Harper and Row, 1965.

003 *Acts: Today's News of the Holy Spirit's Renewal.* Acts Publishers.

004 Adams, Moody P. *Jesus Never Spoke in Tongues.* Privately published, 1974.

005 Adler, Gerhard. *Die Jesus-Bewegung. Aufbruch der enttaüschten Júgend.* Patmos Verlag, 1972.

006 Adorno, T. W., et al. *The Authoritarian Personality.* Harper and Row, 1950.

007 "Against Glossolalia," *Time*, 81 (May 17, 1963): 84.

008 Ageneau, Robert. "Le mouvement pentecotiste catholique," *Spiritus*, 13 (1972): 211-15.

009 Agrimson, J. Elmo, ed. *Gifts of the Spirit and the Body of Christ: Perspectives on the Charismatic Movement.* Augsburg Publishing House, 1974.

010 Aikman, Duncan. "The Holy Rollers," *American Mercury*, 15 (October 1928): 180-91.

011 Alland, Alexander. "Possession in a Revivalistic Negro Church," *Journal for the Scientific Study of Religion*, 1 (1962): 204-13.

012 Allen, Jimmy. "The Corinthian Glossolalia: The Historical Setting, An Exegetical Examination, and a Contemporary Restatement." Unpublished doctor's dissertation, Southern Baptist Theological Seminary, 1967.

013 Allen, Stuart. *Tongues Speaking Today: A Mark of Spirituality or Deception?* Berean Publishing Trust, 1971.

014 Alphanderéry, Paul. "La glossolalie dans le prophétisme mediéval latin," *Revue de l'Historie des Religions*, 104 (November 1931): 417-36.

015 Althaus, Paul. *Communio Sanctorum. Die Gemeinde im lutherischen Kirchengedanken.* Kaiser, 1929.

016 Altmann, Eckhard. *Die Predigt als Kontaktgeschehen.* (Arbeiten zur Theol. 1/13.) Calwer Verlag, 1963.

017 Altrichter, M. "Katholische Pfingstbewegung," *Orientierung*, 36:6 (1972): 70-72.

018 Alvarez de Linera, A. "El glosolalo y su interprete," *Estudios biblicos*, 9 (1950): 193-208.

019 American Lutheran Church. "A Report on Glossolalia," in *Presence, Power, Praise: Documents on the Charismatic Renewal.* 3 vols. Liturgical Press, 1980. 1: 55-63.

020 Amiot, F. "Glossolalie," *Catholicisme*, 5 (1962): 67-69.

021 Anderson, C. "Tongues of Men and Angels," *Lutheran Standard*, (May 16, 1972): 6.

022 Anderson, E. Howard. *Receive the Holy Spirit.* Privately published, n.d.

023 Anderson, Hans Jorgen. *The "A B C" of Acts 2:4. Glosse-Tongues.* Privately published, 1926.

024 Anderson, Mabbette. *The Latter Rain and Its Counterfeit.* Privately published, 1907.

025 Anderson, Robert. *Spirit Manifestation and "the Gift of Tongues."* Loizeaux Brothers, n.d.

026 _____. "A Study of the Theology of the Episcopalians, the Lutherans, and the Pentecostals on the Charismata of the Holy Spirit, Especially as Manifested in Speaking in Tongues and Healing." Unpublished master's thesis, Concordia Theological Seminary, 1964.

027 Anderson, Robert Mapes. *Vision of the Disinherited: The Making of American Pentecostalism.* Oxford University Press, 1979.

028 Anderson, W. B. *Speaking with Tongues.* Privately published, 1908.

029 Andrews, Edward Deming. *The People Called Shakers.* Oxford University Press, 1953.

030 Andrews, Elias. "Ecstasy," in *The Interpreter's Dictionary of the Bible*, George Arthur Buttrick, editor. 4 vols. Abingdon Press, 1962. A-D: 21-22.

031 _____. "Spiritual Gifts," in *The Interpreter's Dictionary of the Bible*, George Arthur Buttrick, editor. 4 vols. Abingdon Press, 1962. R-Z: 435-37.

032 _____. "Tongues, Gift of," in *The Interpreter's Dictionary of the Bible*, George Arthur Buttrick, editor. 4 vols. Abingdon Press, 1962. R-Z: 671-72.

033 Ansons, Gunars. "The Charismatics and Their Churches: Report on Two Conferences," in *Dialog*, 15:2 (1976): 142-44.

034 Appia, Georges. "Une nouvelle Pentecôte," *Unité chrétienne*, 28 (1972): 53-56.

035 Archer, Antony. "Teach Yourself Tongue-Speaking," *New Blackfriars*, 55:651 (August 1974): 357-64.

036 Argue, A. H. *Is Speaking in Tongues an Essential Sign?* The Pentecostal Herald, 1919.

037 Argue, Zelma. *What Meaneth This? The Story of Our Personal Experiences and Evangelistic Campaigns: The Argue Evangelistic Party*. Privately published, 1924.

038 Arndt, Johann. *Johann Arndts Sechs Bücher vom Wahren Christentum nebst dessen Parodies-Gärtlein*. 13th ed. Steinkopf Verlag, n.d.

039 Arnold, Gottfried. *Unparteiische Kirchen-und Ketzerhistorie vom Anfang des Neuen Testaments bis uf das Jahr Christi 1688*. 2 vols. Olms, 1967.

040 Arnot, Arthur B. "The Modern 'Speaking with Tongues,' " *The Evangelical Christian*, 46 (January 1950): 23-25, 59.

041 Arrington, French L. "The Indwelling, Baptism, and Infilling with the Holy Spirit: A Differentiation of Terms," *Pneuma*, 3:2 (Fall 1981): 1-10.

042 Arthur, William. *Tongues of Fire*. Harper and Brothers, 1856.

043 Ashcraft, Jessie Morris. "Glossolalia in the First Epistle to the Corinthians," in *Tongues*, Luther B. Dyer, editor. LeRoi Publishers, 1971. Pp. 60-84.

044 _____. "Speaking in Tongues in the Book of Acts," in *Tongues*, Luther B. Dyer, editor. LeRoi Publishers, 1971. Pp. 85-104.

045   Assemblies of God, General Council. "Minutes of the Annual Meet-
      ing of the Assemblies of God in the U.S.A., Canada and Foreign
      Lands." Vols. 1-9 (1914-1921).

046   _____. "Minutes of the Biennial Meeting. . . ." Vols. 10-17
      (1923-1937).

047   _____. "Minutes of the Executive Presbyters," (1946).

048   Assemblies of God, Kansas District Council. "The Harvester: His-
      tory of the Kansas District Council, 1913-1955." (ca. 1955).

049   Assemblies of God, Public Relations Department. "Early History of
      the Assemblies of God." Assemblies of God, International
      Headquarters, 1959.

050   Associaçõ de Seminários Teológicos Evangélicos (ASTE). *O Espír-
      ito Santo e o Movimento Pentecostal, Simpósio.* ASTE, 1966.

051   Atter, Gordon. *The Third Force.* The Book Nook, 1962.

052   Aufbruch, Der. *Charismatische Erneuerung in de Katholischen
      Kirche.* Kühne, 1973.

053   "The Augsburg Confession in the United States," *Currents in The-
      ology and Missions* (July 2, 1980).

054   Axup, Edward J. *The Truth About Bible Tongues.* Privately pub-
      lished, 1933.

B

055 Bach, Marcus. *The Inner Ecstasy*. Abingdon Press, 1969.

056 _____. "Whether There Be 'Tongues,' " *Christian Herald*, 87 (May 1964): 10-11, 20, 22.

057 von Baer, Heinrich. *Der heilige Geist in den Lukasschriften*. Verlag von W. Kohlhammer, 1962.

058 Baer, Richard A. "Quaker Silence, Catholic Liturgy, and Pentecostal Glossolalia—Some Functional Similarities," in *Perspectives on the New Pentecostalism*, Russell F. Spittler, editor. Baker Book House, 1976. Pp. 150-64.

059 Baëta, C. G. *Prophetism in Ghana: A Study of Some "Spiritual" Churches*. SCM Press, 1962.

060 Baker, Cheryl Diane. "A Psycho-Political Comparison of Hallucinatory Phenomena Amongst Schizophrenics, LSD Users and Glossolalics." Unpublished master's thesis, University of Witwatersrand, 1983.

061 Baker, D. L. "An Interpretation of 1 Corinthians 12-14," *Evangelical Quarterly*, 46 (October-December 1974): 224-34.

062 Baker, J. B. "A Theological Look at the Charismatic Movement," *Churchman*, 86 (Winter 1972): 259-77.

063 Baker, John. *Baptized in One Spirit*. Logos International, n.d.

064 _____. *Baptized in One Spirit: The Meaning of 1 Corinthians 12:13*. Fountain Trust, 1967.

065 Banks, R. M. "Speaking in Tongues: A Survey of the New Testament Evidence," *Churchman*, 80 (1966): 287-94.

066 Banks, William L. *Questions You Have Always Wanted to Ask about Tongues*. American Mission to the Greeks, 1978.

067 *The Baptism with the Holy Ghost and Fire*. Gospel Publishing House, n.d.

068 Barbarie, T. "Tongues, sí, Latin, no," *Triumph*, 4 (April 1, 1969): 20-22.

069 Barber, Theodore X. "Multidimensional Analysis of 'Hypnotic Behavior,' " *Journal of Abnormal Psychology*, 74 (1969): 209-20.

070 Barde, E. "La Glossolalie," *Revue de théologie at des Questions religieuses*, 5 (1896): 125-38.

071 Barfoot, Charles H. and Gerald T. Shepherd. "Prophetic vs. Priestly Religion: The Changing Role of Women Clergy in Classical Pentecostal Churches," *Review of Religious Research*, 22 (1980): 2-17.

072 Barnes, Douglas. "Charisma and Religious Leadership: An Historical Analysis," *Journal for the Scientific Study of Religion*, 17 (March 1978): 1-18.

073 Barnett, Maurice. "The Gift of the Spirit in the New Testament, with Special Reference to Glossolalia." Unpublished master's thesis, University of Manchester, 1946.

074 _____. *The Living Flame: Being a Study of the Gift of the Spirit in the New Testament, with Special Reference to Prophecy, Glossolalia, Montanism and Perfectionism*. Epworth Press, 1953.

075 Barnhart, Joe E. *The Billy Graham Religion*. Pilgrim Press, 1972.

076 Barnhouse, Donald Grey. "Finding Fellowship with Pentecostals," *Eternity*, 9 (April 1958): 8-10.

077 Barratt, Thomas Ball. *In the Days of the Latter Rain*. Simpkin, Marshall, Hamilton, Kent, 1909.

078 _____. *The Truth about the Pentecostal Revival*. Nisbet, 1908.

079 _____. *When the Fire Fell, or God's Dealings With One of His Children*, 1907; reprinted under *When the Fire Fell, and an Outline of My Life*. 2nd ed. Larvik, 1927.

080 Barrett, David B. *Schism and Renewal in Africa: An Analysis of Six Thousand Contemporary Religious Movements*. Oxford University Press, 1968.

081 Bartleman, Frank. *Around the World by Faith*. Privately published, n.d.

082 _____. *Azusa Street*. Logos International, 1980.

083 _____. *How Pentecost Came to Los Angeles*. 2nd ed. Privately published, 1925.

084 ———. *What Really Happened at Azusa Street?* Voice Christian Publications, 1962.

085 Bartling, V. A. "Notes on Spirit-Baptism and Prophetic Utterance," *Concordia Theological Monthly*, 39 (November 1968): 708-14.

086 Bartling, W. J. "Congregation of Christ: A Charismatic Body: An Exegetical Study of 1 Corinthians 12," *Concordia Theological Monthly*, 40 (February 1969): 67-80.

087 Barton, George A. *Archaeology and the Bible*. American Sunday School Union, 1916.

088 *Bases bibliques de l'Eglise Evangélique de La Chaux-de-Fonds*, (folder, Eglise Evangélique de Réveil, La Chaux-de-Fonds, Switzerland, n.d.)

089 Basham, Don. "Baptism in the Holy Spirit," in *The Holy Spirit in Today's Church*, Erling Jorstad, editor. Abingdon Press, 1973. Pp. 58-65.

090 ———. *A Handbook of Holy Spirit Baptism*. Whitaker Books, 1969.

091 ———. *A Handbook on Tongues, Interpretations and Prophecy*. Whitaker Books, 1971.

092 ———. *A Manual for Spiritual Warfare*. Manna Books, 1974.

093 ———. *The Miracle of Tongues*. Revell, 1973.

094 ———. "I Saw My Church Come to Life," *Christian Life*, 26 (March 1965): 37-39.

095 ———. "Speaking in Tongues," in *The Holy Spirit in Today's Church*, Erling Jorstad, editor. Abingdon Press, 1973. Pp. 77-87.

096 ———. "They Dared to Believe," *Christian Life*, 28 (April 1967): 28, 52-56.

097 Bauer, W. "Über die Sprachengabe und über das "glōssais lalein." Denkschrift des Seminars zu Herborn, 1842.

098 Baum, William W. "The Holy Spirit and Prayer." Unpublished Pastoral Letter, July 14, 1974.

099 Bauman, C. "Manifestations of the Spirit of God on Charismatic Movement," in *The New Way of Jesus*, William Klassen, editor. Faith and Life Press, 1980. Pp. 135-47.

100 Bauman, Louis S. *The Tongues Movement*. Brethren Missionary Herald, 1963.

101 Baur, F. C. "Kritische Übersicht über die neuesten des *glōssais lalein* in der ersten christlichen Kirche betreffend der Untersuchung," *Theologische Studien und Kritiken*, 2 (1838): 618-702.

102 _____. "Über den wahren Begriff des *glōssais lalein*," *Zeitschrift für Theologie*, 3 (1830): 78-133.

103 Baxendale, Richard. "The Pentecostal Movement: Does It Matter?" *The Clergy Review*, 52 (January 1967): 9-19.

104 Baxter, J. Sidlow. *His Deeper Work in Us*. Zondervan, 1974.

105 Baxter, Robert. *Narrative of Facts Characterizing the Supernatural Manifestations in Members of Mr. Irving's Congregation*. Nisbet, 1833.

106 Beacham, Paul F. *Scriptural Sanctification*. Advocate Publishing House, 9th ed., n.d.

107 Beardsley, Frank Grenville. *A History of American Revivals*. American Tract Society, 1904.

108 Beare, Frank W. "Speaking with Tongues," *Journal of Biblical Literature*, 83 (September 1964): 229-46.

109 Beattie, J. and J. Middleton, eds. *Spirit Mediumship and Society in Africa*. Routledge and Kegan Paul, 1969.

110 Beauclerc, J. "A travers les revues," *Études*, 123 (1910): 867-71.

111 Becken, Hans-Jürgen. *Theologie der Heilung: Das Heilung in den Afrikanischen Unabhängigen Kirchen in Südafrika*. Verlag der Missionshandlung, 1972.

112 Becker, Wilhard, "Die Charismen in der evangelischen Kirche heute," in *Kirche und Chrisma*, Reiner Edel, editor. 1975. Pp. 157-67.

113 Beckmann, David M. "Trance: From Africa to Pentecostalism," *Concordia Theological Monthly*, 45 (January 1974): 11-26.

114 Beeg, John Frederick. "Beliefs and Values of Charismatics: A Survey." Unpublished doctor's dissertation, Colgate Rochester Divinity School, 1978.

115 Beel, A. "Donum linguarum jukta Act. Apost. ii. 1-13," *Collationes*, 35 (1935): 417-20.

116 Behm, Johannes. "γλῶσσα," in *Theological Dictionary of the New Testament*, Gerhard Kittel, editor. Trans. Geoffrey W. Bromiley. 10 vols. Eerdmans, 1964-1976. 1: 719-27.

117 Belew, Pascal P. *Light on the Tongues Question*. Nazarene Publishing House, 1926.

118 Bell, Henry. "Speaking in Tongues." Unpublished doctor's dissertation, Evangelical Theological College, 1930.

119 Bell, L. Nelson. "Babel of Pentecost," *Christianity Today*, 4 (October 12, 1959): 19.

120 Bellah, Robert N. *The Broken Covenant*. The Seabury Press, 1975.

121 Bellshaw, William G. "The Confusion of Tongues," *Bibliotheca Sacra*, 120 (April-June 1963): 145-53.

122 Benner, P. D. "The Universality of Tongues," *The Japan Christian Quarterly*, 39 (Spring 1973): 101-107.

123 Bennett, Dennis. "The Charismatic Renewal and Liturgy," *View*, 2:1 (1965): 1-6.

124 _____. "The Gifts of The Holy Spirit," in *The Charismatic Movement*, Michael Hamilton, editor. Eerdmans, 1975. Pp. 15-32.

125 _____. "The New Pentecost Charismatic Revival Seminar Report." Full Gospel Business Men's Fellowship International, 1963.

126 _____. *Nine O'Clock in the Morning*. Logos International, 1970.

127 _____. "Pentecost: When Episcopalians Start Speaking in Tongues," *The Living Church*, 142 (January 1, 1961): 12-13.

128 _____. "They Spake with Tongues and Magnified God!" *Full Gospel Business Men's Voice*, 8 (October 1960): 6-8.

129 _____. *When Episcopalians Start Speaking in Tongues*. Christian Retreat Center, n.d.

130 Bennett, Dennis and Rita Bennett. *The Holy Spirit and You*. Logos International, 1971.

131 Benz, Ernst. *Der Heilige Geist in Amerika*. Diederichs, 1970.

132 _____, ed. *Messianische Kirchen, Sekten und Bewegungen im heutigen Afrika*. E. J. Brill, 1965.

133 Berg, Daniel. *Enviado por Deus, Memórias de Daniel Berg*. AdD, 1959.

134 Berg, Horst Klaus. "Die Religion der Jesus-people," *Katechatische Blätter*, 97 (1972): 735-50.

135 Berger, Alan L. "Hasidism and Moonism: Charisma in the Counterculture," *Sociological Analysis*, 41 (Winter 1980): 375-90.

136 Berger, Peter L. "Sectarianism and Religious Sociation," *The American Journal of Sociology*, 64 (1958): 41-44.

137 Bergquist, Susan L. "The Revival of Glossolalic Practices in the Catholic Church: Its Sociological Implications," *Perkins Journal*, 30 (1973): 256-65.

138 Bergsma, Stuart. *Speaking with Tongues: Some Physiological and Psychological Implications of Modern Glossolalia*. Baker Book House, 1965.

139 _____. "Speaking with Tongues," *Torch and Trumpet*, 14 (November 1964): 8-11.

140 _____. "Speaking with Tongues," *Torch and Trumpet*, 14 (December 1964): 9-13.

141 Berkhof, Hendrikus. *The Doctrine of the Holy Spirit*. John Knox Press, 1964.

142 Bernstein, B. "Linguistic Codes, Hesitation Phenomena, and Intelligence," *Language and Speech*, 5 (1962): 31-46.

143 Bertrand, Philippe. "Expressions récontes du mouvement charismatique aux Etats-Unis," *Amitié*, 4 (1973): 33-35.

144 Bésnard, Albert N. "La prisme des opinions," *Vie Spirituelle* 128 (January-February 1974): 6-22.

145 Bess, Donovan. "Speaking in Tongues—the High Church Heresy," *The Nation*, 197 (September 28, 1963): 173-77.

146 Bess, S. Herbert. "The Office of the Prophet in Old Testament Times," *Grace Journal*, 1 (Spring 1960): 7-12.

147 Besson, Henri. *Le mouvement de sanctification et le réveil d'Oxford*. Neuchâtel, 1914.

148 Best, Ernest. "The Interpretation of Tongues," *Scottish Journal of Theology*, 28:1 (1975): 45-62.

149 Beuson, Frank. "A Story of Division," in *The Charismatic Movement*, Michael Hamilton, editor. Eerdmans, 1975. Pp. 185-94.

150 Bhengu, Nicholas B. H., *Revival Fire in South Africa*. Afro-American Missionary Crusade, Inc., n.d. (ca. 1949).

151 Bibra, O. S. von. *Die Bevollmächtigten des Christus. Das Wesen ihres Dienstes im Lichte des Neuen Testamentes. Eine Untersuchung über die Kennzeichen der ecten Diener m Wort nach dem Neuen Testament*. Schriftenmissions-Verlag, 1947.

152 "Billy Graham on the Jesus Generation," *Life and Work*, 28:5 (1972): 10-11.

153 Bird, Thomas. "Experience over Scripture in Charismatic Exegesis," *Concordia Theological Quarterly*, 45:1-2 (January-April 1981): 5-11.

154 Bishop, Albert E. *Tongues, Signs, and Visions Not God's Order for Today*. Moody Press, n.d.

155 Bishop, Richard W. *An Investigation of the Relationship of the Baptism in the Spirit to the Devotional Life of Charismatic Christians*, North American Baptist Seminary, 1982.

156 Bittlinger, Arnold. *Das Abendmahl im Neuen Testament und in der fruhen Kirche*. Kühne Verlag, 1969.

157 _____. "Die Bedeutung der Charismen für den Gemeindeaufbau," in *Bedeutung*. Edel, 1964. Pp. 5-18.

158 _____. *Die Bedeutung der Gnadengaben für die Gemeinde Jesu Christi*. Edel, 1964.

159 _____. *Charisma und Amt*. Calwer Verlag, 1947.

160 _____. "Charismatic Renewal: An Opportunity for the Church?" *The Ecumenical Review*, 31:3 (July 1979): 247-51.

161 _____. "A Charismatic Worship Service in the New Testament Today," *Studia Liturgica*, 9:4 (1973): 215-29.

162 _____. "Die charismatische Erneuerung der Kirchen: Aufbruch urchristlichen Erfahrung," in *Erfahrung und Theologie des Heiligen, Geists,* C. Heitmann and H. Mühle, editors. Kössel, 1974. Pp. 19-35

163 _____, ed. *The Church Is Charismatic*. World Council of Churches, 1981.

164 _____. "Disziplinierte Charismen," *Deutsches Pfarrerblatt*, 63 (1963): 333f.

165 _____. *Der fruhchristliche Gottesdienst und sein Wiederbelebung innerhalf der reformatorischen Kirchen der Gegenwart*, (Oekumenische Texte und Studien 30). Edel, 1964.

166 _____. *Gemeinde ist Anders: Verwirklichung neutestamentliche Gemeindeordnung innerbalb der Volkskirche*. Calwer Verlag, 1966.

167 _____. "Gemeinde und Charisma," *Das missionarische Wort*, 17 (1964): 231-35.

168 _____. *Gifts and Graces: A Commentary on 1 Corinthians 12-14*. Eerdmans, 1967.

169 _____. *Gifts and Ministries*. Eerdmans, 1973; Hodder & Stoughton, 1974.

170 _____. *Glossolalia: Wert und Problematik des Sprachenredens*. Kühne, 1966.

171 ————. "Die Gnadengaben in der Bibel (1 Kor. 12.7-11)", in *Bedeutung*. Edel, 1964. Pp. 24-47.

172 ————. *Gnadengaben. Eine Auslegung von 1 Kor. 12-14*. Edel, 1966.

173 ————. *Gottesdienst Heute*. Calwer Verlag, 1968.

174 ————. "Et ils prient en d'autres langues: le movement charismatique et la glossolalie," *Foi et Vie*, 72:4/5 (1973): 97-108.

175 ————. *Im Kraftfeld des Heiligen Geistes*. Edel, 1974.

176 ————. *Liebe und Charisma. Eine Besinnung über 1 Kor. 13*. Rufer-Zentrale, 1965.

177 ————. *Papst und Pfingstler. Der römisch katholisch-pfingstliche Dialog und seine ökumenische Relevanz*. Peter Lang, 1978.

178 ————. "Report on the Work of the WCC Consultant on Charismatic Renewal," in *The Church is Charismatic: The World Council of Churches and the Charismatic Renewal*, edited by Arnold Bittlinger. World Council of Churches, 1981.

179 ————. *Und sie beten in anderen Sprachen: Charismatische Bewegung und Glossolalie*. Ökumenischer Schriftendienst 2. Wetzhausen, 1972.

180 ————. *Das Sprachenreden in der Kirch. Seine Bedeutung und Problematik in Vergangenheit und Gegenwart*. Edel, 1962.

181 Bittlinger, Arnold and Kilian McDonnell. *Baptism in the Holy Spirit as an Ecumenical Problem*. Charismatic Renewal Services, 1972.

182 Bixler, Russell. *It Can Happen to Anybody*. Whitaker Books, 1970.

183 ————. "Speaking in Tongues—Glossolalia: A Response," *Brethren Life and Thought*, 21 (Winter 1976): 51-58.

184 Bjerre, Martinus. *Feg fik det i tilgift*. Den Apostolske Kirkes Forlag, n.d.

185 Björkquist, Curt. *Den Svenska pingstväckelsen*. Förlaget Filadelfia, 1959.

186 Bjørner, Anna Larsen. *Teater og Tempel. Livserindringer*. H. Hirschsprungs Forlag, 1935.

187 Blackwelder, Boyce W. "Thirty Errors of Modern Tongues Advocates," *Vital Christianity*, 94 (May 26, 1974): 9-10.

188 Blakemore, W. B. "Holy Spirit as Public and as Charismatic Institutions," *Encounter*, 36 (Summer 1975): 161-80.

189 Blaney, Harvey J. S. "St. Paul's Posture on Speaking in Unknown Tongues," *Wesley Theological Journal*, 8 (1973): 52-60.

190 Bleek, F. "Noch ein Paar Worte über die Gbe des *glōssais lalein*," *Theologische Studien und Kritiken*, 3 (1830): 45-64.

191 _____. "Über die Gabe des *glōssais lalein* in der ersten christlichen Kirche," *Theologische Studien und Kritiken*, 2 (1829): 3-79.

192 Blessitt, Arthur. *Tell the World: A Jesus People Manual*. Privately published, 1972.

193 _____. *Turned on to Jesus*. Hawthorne Books, 1971.

194 Blikstad, Vernon M. "Spiritual Renaissance," *Christian Life*, 26 (May 1964): 31.

195 Bloch-Hoell, Nils. "Den Heilige and I Pinsebevegelsen, den Charismatiske Beveglse og I Jesus-Vekkelsen," *Nederlands Theologisch Tijdschrift*, 77:2 (1976): 75-86.

196 _____. "Der Heilige Geist in der Pfingstbewegung und in der charismaischen Bewegung," in *Taufe und Heiliger Geist*, Pertti Mäki, editor. Helsinki Press, 1979. Pp. 89-105.

197 _____. *The Pentecostal Movement: Its Origin, Development, and Distinctive Character*. Allen and Unwin, 1964.

198 _____. *Pinsebevegelsen*. University of Oslo Press, 1956.

199 Bloesch, Donald G. "The Charismatic Revival," *Religion in Life*, 35 (Summer 1966): 364-80.

200 _____. *The Evangelical Renaissance*. Eerdmans, 1973.

201 _____. *Wellsprings of Renewal: Promise in Christian Communal Life*. Eerdmans, 1974.

202 Blossom, Willis W. *The Gift of the Holy Spirit*. Privately published, 1925.

203 Bloy, Myron B., Jr. *Search for the Sacred: The New Spiritual Quest*. The Seabury Press, 1972.

204 "Blue Tongues," *Time*, 81 (March 29, 1963): 52.

205 Blumhardt, Joh. *Zuverlässiger Abdruck seines eigenen Berichtes über die Krankheits- und Heilungsgeschichte der Gottliebin Dittus in Möttlingen*, (mit einer Einführung von Prof. W. Koller). Erlangen, 1955.

206 Bobon, Jean. "Les Pseudo-Glossolalies Ludiques et Magiques," *Journal of Belge de Neurologie et de Psychiatrie*, 47 (April 1947): 219ff.

207 Boer, Harry R. "The Spirit: Tongues and Message," *Christianity Today*, 7 (January 4, 1963): 6-7.

208 Boerwinkel, F. *De Pinkstergroepen*, (Oekumenische Leergang No. 5). Plein, 1963.

209 Bois, Henri. *Le Reveil au Pays de Galles*. Delachaux et Niestlé, 1905.

210 Boisen, Anton T. "Economic Distress and Religious Experience," *Psychiatry*, 2 (1939): 185-94.

211 _____. *The Exploration of the Inner World*. Harper and Row, 1936.

212 _____. *Religion in Crisis and Custom: A Sociological and Psychological Study*. Harper and Row, 1955.

213 _____. "Religion and Hard Times: A Study of the Holy Rollers," *Social Action*, 5 (March 15, 1939): 8-35.

214 Boisset, L. *Mouvement de Jésus et Renouveau dans l'Esprit*. Centre Théologique de Meylan, 1975.

215 Bond, Georgia. *Life Story of the Rev. O. H. Bond*. Privately published, 1958.

216 Bond, J. Max. "The Negro in Los Angeles." Unpublished doctor's dissertation, University of Southern California, 1936.

217 Borchert, Bruno. "Jesus-Movement," *Concilium*, 79 (1972): 101-105.

218 Bord, Richard J. and Joseph E. Faulkner. *The Catholic Charismatics: Anatomy of a Modern Religious Movement*. Pennsylvania State University Press, 1984.

219 _____. "Religiosity and Secular Attitudes: The Case of Catholic Pentecostals," *Journal for the Scientific Study of Religion*, 14 (September 1975): 257-70.

220 Boros, Ladislaus. "Discernment of the Spirit," in *Charisms in the Church*, Christian Duquoc and Casiano Floristan, editors. The Seabury Press, 1978. Pp. 78-86.

221 Bosworth, Fred F. *Do All Speak with Tongues?* Christian Alliance Publishing Company, n.d.

222 Bouchet, Jean-René. "The Discernment of Spirits," in *Conflicts About the Holy Spirit*, Hans Küng and Jürgen Moltmann, editors. The Seabury Press, 1979. Pp. 103-106.

223 Bourguignon, Erika, ed. *Religion, Altered States of Consciousness and Social Change*. Ohio State University Press, 1973.

224 _____. "World Distribution and Patterns of Possession States," in *Trance and Possession States*, Raymond Prince, editor. R. M. Bucke Memorial Society, 1968. Pp. 3-34.

225 Bourguignon, E. and A. Haas. "Transcultural Research and Culture-Bound Psychiatry." Paper presented at the Western Division Meeting of the American Psychiatrical Association, Honolulu, 1965.

226 Bourguignon, E. and L. Pettay. "Spirit Possession, Trance and Cross-Cultural Research." Unpublished paper, Ohio State University, 1966.

227 Bouyer, Louis. "Some Charismatic Movements in the History of the Church," in *Perspectives on Chrismatic Renewal*, Edward D. O'Connor, editor. University of Notre Dame Press, 1975. Pp. 113-31.

228 _____. *History of Spirituality*. Burns and Oates, 1969.

229 Bovet, P. "Le parler en langues des premies chrétiens," *Revue d'histoire des religions*, 63/64 (1911): 292-310.

230 Bowen, T. M. *Why We Baptize in Jesus' Name*. Pentecostal Publishing House, n.d.

231 Boyd, Frank M. *The Holy Spirit: Teachers' Manual*. Gospel Publishing House, n.d.

232 Boyer, James L. "An Exposition of 1 Corinthians." Unpublished classroom notes, Grace Theological Seminary, 1964.

233 _____. "The Office of the Prophet in New Testament Times," *Grace Journal*, 1 (Spring 1960): 13-20.

234 Bozzano, Ernesto. *Polyglot Mediumship*. Rider and Company, 1932.

235 Bracco, Roberto. *Il risveglio pentecostale in Italia*. Privately published, n.d.

236 Bradfield, Cecil David. "He's Not One Of Us—Yet: Research in a Neo-Pentecostal Group," *Pneuma*, 1:1 (Spring 1979): 49-57.

237 _____. *Neo-Pentecostalism: A Sociological Assessment*. University Press of America, 1979.

238 Bradford, George C. "Are Presbyterians Post-Pentecostals?" *Presbyterian Life*, 21 (June 1, 1968): 30.

239 Brandt, R. L. "The Case for Speaking in Tongues," *Pentecostal Evangel*, 48 (June 5, 1960): 4, 29-30.

240 ———. "Tongues . . . For A Sign," *The Pentecostal Evangel*, (April 26, 1964): 3-5.

241 Branick, Vincent P. *Mary: The Spirit and the Church*. Paulist Press 1980.

242 Bray, A. E. *Revolt of the Protestants of the Cevennes*. Murray, 1870.

243 Brecht, Martin. "Christentum als Lebensordnung. Die Frömmigkeit des Pietismus," in *Evangelischer Glaube im Wandel der Zeit*. Steinkopf Verlag, 1967.

244 Breckenridge, James F. *The Theological Self-Understanding of the Catholic Charismatic Movement*. University Press of America, 1980.

245 Bredesen, Harald. "Discovery at Hillside," *Christian Life*, 20 (January 1959): 16-18.

246 ———. "Discovery at Yale," *Trinity*, 1 (Christmastide 1962-1963): 15-17.

247 ———. "The Foolish Things," *Trinity*, 2 (Trinitytide 1962): 2-3.

248 ———. "Return to the Charismata," *Trinity*, 2 (Whitsuntide 1962): 22.

249 ———. *Yes, Lord*. Logos International, 1972.

250 Bresson, Bernard L. *Studies in Ecstasy*. Vantage Press, 1966.

251 Brewster, Percy S. *Der Dienst der Krankenheilung in de Kirche— Möglichkeit oder Verpflichtung?* Edel, 1964.

252 ———, ed. *Pentecostal Doctrine*. Grenehurst Press, 1976.

253 ———. *The Spreading Flame of Pentecost*. Elim Publishing Company, 1970.

254 Brice, Joseph Isaac. *Pentecost*. Hodder & Stoughton, 1936.

255 Bridge, Donald and David Phypers. *Spiritual Gifts and the Church*. Inter-Varsity Press, 1973.

256 Briem, Efraim. "Charismatic Christians Seek to Infuse the Faith with Their Joyous Spirit," *The New York Times*, (July 22, 1977): 1.

257 ———. "Den evangeliska kyrkan och de nutida väckelserörelserna," in *Protokoll vid nordiska prästmötet i Helsingfors 1933*. Helsinki 1933.

258 ———. *Den moderna pingströrelsen*. Svenska Diakonistyrelses Bokförlag, 1924.

259 Britten, E. H. *Modern American Spiritualism*. Privately published, 1870.

260 Britton, Francis M. *Pentecostal Truth*. Publishing House of the Pentecostal Holiness Church, 1919.

261 Broadbent, W. G. *The Doctrine of Tongues*. Eldon Press, n.d.

262 Broek, A. "Jesus Movement wordt Jezus de Man-van-het jaar?" *Jeugden Samenleving*, 2 (1972): 17-29.

263 Brown, Charles E. *The Confusion of Tongues*. Gospel Trumphet Company, 1949.

264 Brown, Colin. *The Charismatic Contribution: How Significant Is the Charismatic Movement*. New Zealand Press, 1980.

265 Brown, Dale. *Flamed by the Spirit: Biblical Definition of the Holy Spirit*. Brethren Press, 1978.

266 Brown, L. B. "Some Attitudes Surrounding Glossolalia," *Colloquium*, 2 (1967): 221-28.

267 _____. "The Structure of Religious Belief," *Journal for the Scientific Study of Religion*, 5 (1966): 259-72.

268 Brumback, Carl. *Suddenly From Heaven*. Gospel Publishing House, 1961.

269 _____. *What Meaneth This? A Pentecostal Answer to a Pentecostal Question*. Gospel Publishing House, 1947.

270 Bruner, Benjamin Harrison. *Pentecost: A Renewal of Power*. Doubleday, Doran and Company, 1928.

271 Bruner, Frederick Dale. *The Doctrine and Experience of the Holy Spirit in the Pentecostal Movement and Correspondingly in the New Testament*. Unpublished doctor's dissertation, University of Hamburg, 1963.

272 _____. *A Theology of the Holy Spirit: The Pentecostal Experience and the New Testament Witness*. Eerdmans, 1970.

273 Brunner, Peter. "Charismatische und Methodische Schriftauslegung nach Augustins Prolog zu de Doctrina Christiana," *Kerygma und Dogma*, 1 (1955): 59-69, 85-103.

274 Bryant, Ernest and Daniel O'Connell. "A Phonemic Analysis of Nine Samples of Glossolalic Speech," *Psychonomic Speech*, 22 (1971): 81-83.

275 Buchanan, Colin. "Baptism in the Holy Spirit," *Churchman*, 86 (1972): 39-46.

276   Buck, E. Parker. *The True Bible Teaching Versus the Unknown Tongue Theory*. Privately published, n.d.

277   Buckles, Ernest A. *A Brief History: The Church of God [of the Apostolic Faith]*. Privately published, 1935.

278   Budd, William H. *The Bible Gift of Tongues*. Pentecostal Publishing House, 1909.

279   Bundy, David. "Historical Perspectives on the Development of the European Pentecostal Theological Association," *Pneuma*, 2:2 (Fall 1980): 15-25.

280   Bunn, John T. "Glossolalia in Historical Perspective," in *Speaking in Tongues: Let's Talk about It*, Watson E. Mills, editor. Word Books, 1973. Pp. 36-47.

281   Burdick, Donald W. *Tongues: To Speak or Not to Speak!* Moody Press, 1969.

282   Burgess, Stanley M. "Medieval Examples of Charismatic Piety in the Roman Catholic Church," in *Pespectives on the New Pentecostalism*, Russell F. Spittler, editor. Baker Book House, 1976. Pp. 14-26.

283   Burgess, W. J. *Glossolalia: Speaking in Tongues*. Baptist Publications Committee, 1968.

284   Burke, Kathryn L. and Merlin B. Brinkerhoff, "Capturing Charisma: Notes on an Elusive Concept," *Journal for the Scientific Study of Religion*, 20 (1981): 274-84.

285   Burkett, Randall K. and Richard Newman. *Black Apostles: Afro-American Clergy Confront the Twentieth Century*. G. K. Hall, 1978.

286   Burns, J. Lanier. "Reemphasis on the Purpose of the Sign Gifts," *Bibliotheca Sacra*, 132 (July-September 1975): 242-49.

287   Byrne, James. *Threshold of God's Promise: An Introduction to the Catholic Pentecostal Movement*. Ave Maria Press, 1970.

288   Byrum, Russel R. *Holy Spirit Baptism and the Second Cleansing*. Gospel Trumpet Company, 1923.

C

289 Caffarel, H. *Faut-il parler d'un Pentecótisme catholique?* Editions du Renouveau, 1973.

290 Cain, Kenneth. *Fresh Wind of the Spirit.* Abingdon Press, 1975.

291 Caldwell, William. *Pentecostal Baptism.* Miracle Moments Evangelistic Association, 1963.

292 Calley, Malcolm J. "Aboriginal Pentecostalism: A Study of Changes in Religion." 4 vols. Unpublished master's thesis, University of Sydney, 1955.

293 _____. *God's People: West Indian Pentecostal Sects in England.* Oxford University Press, 1965.

294 Campbell, James A. *After Pentecost What?* Revell, 1897.

295 _____. "A Speaking Acquaintance with Tongues." Unpublished paper, University of Pittsburg, 1965.

296 Campbell, Joseph E. *The Pentecostal Holiness Church, 1898-1948.* The Publishing House of the Pentecostal Holiness Church, 1951.

297 _____. *Warning! Do Not Seek for Tongues: A Sound Scriptural Appraisal of a Present-Day Trend in the Church.* World Outlook Publications, 1970.

298 Cantelon, Willard. *The Baptism of the Holy Spirit.* Gospel Publishing House, 1957.

299 Canty, George. *In My Father's House: Pentecostal Expositions of Major Christian Truths.* Attic Press, 1969.

300 Capon, John. *And There Was Light: The Story of the Nationwide Festival of Light.* Lutterworth Press, 1972.

301 Carlson, A. "Tongues of Fire Revisited." Unpublished paper, University of California, 1967.

302 Carmen, Calvin. "The Posture of Pentecostalism in View of the Crucial Issues of the Fundamentalist—Neo-Evangelical Debate." Unpublished master's thesis, Central Bible Institute, 1965.

303 Carr, Wesley. "Towards a Contemporary Theology of the Holy Spirit," *Scottish Journal of Theology*, 28:6 (1975): 501-16.

304 Carroll, R. Leonard. "Glossolalia: Apostles to the Reformation," in *The Glossolalia Phenomenon*, Wade H. Horton, editor. Pathway Press, 1966. Pp. 69-94.

305 Carter, Charles W. "A Wesleyan View of the Spirit's Gift of Tongues in the Book of Acts," *Wesleyan Theological Journal*, 4 (Spring 1969): 39-68.

306 Carter, Herbert F. *The Spectacular Gifts: Prophecy, Tongues, Interpretations*. Privately published, n.d.

307 Carter, Herbert F. and Ruth K. Moore. "History of the Pentecostal Free Will Baptist Church, Inc.," *The Messenger*, (October 1965): 4.

308 Carter, Howard. *The Gifts of the Spirit*. Northern Gospel Publishing House, 1946.

309 Carter, Richard. "That Old-Time Religion Comes Back," *Coronet*, (February 1958): 125-30.

310 Cate, B. F. *The Nine Gifts of the Spirit Are Not in the Church Today*. Regular Baptist Press, 1957.

311 "Catholic Charismatics: An Age of Revolution," *Christianity Today*, 20 (July 2, 1976): 41-42.

312 "Catholic Pentecostal Movement: Creative or Divisive Enthusiasm?" *Pro Mundi Vita Bulletin*, 60 (May 1976): 3-36.

313 Catrice, P. "Réflexions missionnaires sur la vision de Saint Pierre à Joppé. Du judéo-christianisme a l'Église de tous les peuples," *Bible et Vie Chrétienne*, 79 (1968): 20-39.

314 Cavanar, Jim. "Catholics: Pentecostal Movement," *Acts*, 1 (1968): 14-19.

315 Celles, Charles de. "The Catholic Pentecostal Movement," *Cross and Crown*, 23:4 (1971): 403-16.

316 Cerfaux, L. "La symbolique attachée au miracles des languages," *Emphemerides Theologicae Lovanienses*, 13 (1936): 256-59. Repr. *Recueil Lucien Cerfaux*, 2 (Gemblous 1954): 183-87.

317 Cerullo, Morris. *The New Anointing Is Here*. World Evangelism, 1972.

318 Chadwick, Henry. *Priscillian of Avila: The Occult and the Charismatic in the Early Church*. Clarendon Press, 1976.

319 Chadwick, Samuel. *The Way to Pentecost*. Revell, 1973.

320 Chafer, Lewis Sperry. "The Baptism of the Holy Spirit," *Bibliotheca Sacra*, 109 (1952): 199-216.

321 Chagnon, Roland. *Les charismatiques an Québec*. Québec Amérique, 1979.

322 Chamillard, G. *De Corona Tonsura*. Privately published, 1659.

323 Chandler, Russell. "Charismatic Clinics: Instilling Ministry," *Christianity Today*, 17 (September 28, 1973): 44-45.

324 _____. "Fanning the Charismatic Fire," *Christianity Today*, 12 (November 24, 1967): 39-40.

325 Chantry, Walter J. *Signs of the Apostles: Observations on Pentecostalism Old and New*, rev. ed. Banner of Truth Trust, 1973.

326 Chapman, J. Wilbur. *Received Ye the Holy Ghost?* Revell, 1894.

327 *Charisma Digest*. Full Gospel Business Men's Fellowship International, n.d.

328 "The Charismatic Movement in the Lutheran Church in America." The Commission on Worship of the Lutheran Church in America, 1974.

329 "The Charismatic Movement and Lutheran Theology." A report of the Commission on Theology and Church Relations of the Lutheran Church—Missouri Synod, January 1972.

330 Chéry, H. "Catholiques et Pentecôtistes," *Ecclesia*, 280 (July-August 1972): 10-12.

331 Cheshire, C. Linwood. "The Doctrine of the Holy Spirit in Acts." Unpublished master's thesis, Union Theological Seminary, 1953.

332 Chinn, Jack J. "May We Pentecostals Speak?" *Christianity Today*, 5 (July 17, 1961): 8-9.

333 Chordas, Thomas J. and Stephen J. Cross. "Healing of Memories: Psychotherapeutic Ritual Among Catholic Pentecostals," *Journal of Pastoral Care*, 30 (December 1976): 245-57.

334 Christenson, Larry. "Das Charisma des Zungenredens," in *Die Bedeutung der Gnadengaben*. Edel, 1963. Pp. 72-86.

335 _____. *A Charismatic Approach to Social Action*. Bethany, 1974.

336 _____. *The Charismatic Renewal Among Lutherans*. Bethany, 1976.

337 _____. *Die Gabe des Zungenredens in der Lutherischen Kirche*. Edel, 1963.

338 _____. *The Gift of Tongues*. Privately published, 1963.

339 _____. *A Lutheran Pastor Speaks*. The Blessed Trinity Society, n.d.

340 _____. *A Message to the Charismatic Movement*. Bethany, 1972.

341 _____. "Miracles Are Not Commonplace Here," *Christian Life*, 27 (June 1965): 36-37, 52-54.

342 _____. "Pentecostalism's Forgotten Forerunner," in *Aspects of Pentecostal-Charismatic Origins*, Vinson Synan, editor. Logos International, 1975. Pp. 15-37.

343 _____. *The Renewed Mind*. Bethany, 1974.

344 _____. *Social Action Jesus Style*. Dimension Books, 1976.

345 _____. "Speaking in Tongues," *Trinity*, 2 (November 4, 1963): 15-16.

346 _____. *Speaking in Tongues: A Gift for the Body of Christ*. The Fountain Trust, 1969.

347 _____. *Speaking in Tongues and Its Significance for the Church*. Bethany, 1968.

348 _____, et al. "A Theological and Pastoral Perspective on the Charismatic Renewal in the Lutheran Church." Unpublished paper, 1975.

349 Christie-Murray, David. *Voices from the Gods: Speaking with Tongues*. Routledge and Kegan Paul, 1978.

350 "Church Studies on the Holy Spirit." Documents from the Presbyterian Church of the USA, Church of Scotland, and Presbyterian Church of Canada. Council on Theology and Culture, 1978.

351 Cintron, Pedro. "American Denominational Revivalism and the Pentecostal Movement: A Comparative Study." Unpublished master's thesis, Union Theological Seminary, 1963.

352 Claassen, Arlin. "The Jesus Movement in the Local Community," *Brethren Life and Thought*, 17 (1972): 187-90.

353 Clabaugh, Gary K. *Thunder on the Right: The Protestant Fundamentalit*. Nelson-Hall, 1974.

354 Clark, Elijah C. *The Baptism of the Holy Ghost "And More."* Church of God Publishing House, 1931.

355 Clark, Elmer T. "Modern Speaking with Tongues," in *Twentieth Century Encyclopedia of Religious Knowledge*, L. A. Loetscher, editor. 2 vols. Baker Book House, 1955. 2: 1118.

356 Clark, S. B. *Growing in Faith*. Charismatic Renewal Services, 1972.

357 _____. *Knowing God's Will*. Charismatic Renewal Services, 1972.

358 _____. *Where Are We Headed? Guidelines for the Catholic Charismatic Renewal*. Ave Maria Press, 1973.

359 Clark, Stephen. *Baptized in the Spirit*. Dove Publications, 1970.

360 _____. *Confirmation and the "Baptism of the Holy Spirit."* Dove Publications, 1969.

361 _____. *Spiritual Gifts*. Dove Publications, 1969.

362 Clemen, Carl. "The 'Speaking with Tongues' of the Early Christians," *Expository Times*, 10 (1898): 344-52.

363 Clemens, J. S. "Pentecost," *A Dictionary of the Apostolic Church*, 2 (1908): 160-64.

364 Clément, O. "A propose de l'Espirit-Saint," *Contacts*, 26 (1974): 85-91.

365 Cleveland, Lester. "Let's Demythologize Glossolalia," *The Baptist Program*, 45 (June 1967): 8, 11.

366 Clifford, Richard D. "Street Christians," *The Christian*, 111:10 (1972): 6-7.

367 Cocoris, G. Michael. "Speaking in Tongues: Then and Now," *Biblical Research Quarterly*, 46:6 (September 1981): 14-16.

368 Cohn, Werner. "A Movie of Experimentally-Produced Glossolalia," *Journal for the Scientific Study of Religion*, 6 (1967): 278.

369 _____. "The Paradoxes of Marginal Group: A Social-Psychological Suggestion." Unpublished paper, University of British Columbia, 1967.

370 _____. "Personality and Pentecostal Groups: A Research Note." Unpublished paper, University of British Columbia, 1967.

371 _____. "Personality, Pentecostalism, and Glossolalia: A Research Note on Some Unsuccessful Research," *The Canadian Review of Sociology and Anthropology*, 5 (1968): 36-39.

372 Colletti, Joseph R. "Lewis Pethrus: His Influence Upon Scandinavian-American Pentecostalism" *Pneuma*, 5:2 (Fall 1983): 18-29.

373 Collins, J. D. "Discovering the Meaning of Pentecost," *Scripture*, 20 (1968): 73-79.

374 "Concern over Glossolalia," *Christianity Today*, 7 (May 24, 1963): 30.

375 Conde, Emilio. *Etapas da vida espiritual*. Casa Publicadora da AdD, 1951.

376 _____. *Pentecosts para todos*. Casa Publicadora da AdD, 1951.

377 _____. *O testemunho dos séculos*. Livros Evangélicos, 1960.

378 Congar, Y. M. J. "Actualité renouvelée du Saint-Esprit," *Lumen Vitae*, 27 (1972): 543-60.

379 _____. "La pneumatologie dans la théologie catholique," *Revue des sciences philosophiques et théologiques*, 51 (1972): 250-58.

380 "Congrés du Renouveau charismatique catholique." Participants' brochure for the congress held at Laval University, June 7-9, 1974.

381 Conn, Charles W. "Glossolalia and the Scriptures," in *The Glossolalia Phenomenon*, Wade H. Horton, editor. Pathway Press, 1966. Pp. 23-65.

382 _____. *Like a Mighty Army Moves the Church of God, 1886-1955*. Church of God Publishing House, 1955.

383 _____. *Pillars of Pentecost*. Pathway Press, 1956.

384 _____. "A Spiritual Explosion," *Christian Life*, 28 (July 1966): 30-31, 54.

385 Connelly, James T. "Reviews of Jesus and the Spirit, Charismatic Renewal and the Churches Perspectives on Charismatic Renewal and the New Charismatics," *Horizons*, 4 (Spring 1977): 139, 142-44.

386 "Constitution and By-Laws of the Society for Pentecostal Studies," *Pneuma*, 4:2 (Fall 1982): 46-52.

387 Cook, Glenn A. *The Azusa Street Meeting*. N.p., n.d. (c. 1920).

388 Corcoran, Patrick. "The Holy Spirit and the Life of the Spirit Today," in *The Witness of the Spirit*, Wilfrid Harrington, editor. Irish Biblical Association, 1979. Pp. 97-111.

389 Corvin, R. O. "History of the Educational Institutions of the Pentecostal Holiness Church." Unpublished doctor's dissertation, Southwestern Baptist Theological Seminary, 1956.

390 Cossec, C. le. *Le Saint-Esprit et les dons spirituels. Toute la vérité concernant le surnaturel divin.* (Vérité à connaître 3.) Privately published, n.d.

391 _____. *Le vrai Baptême. L'Eglise. La sanctification.* (Vérité à connaître 2.) Privately published, n.d.

392 Coulson, Jesse E. "Glossolalia and Internal-External Locus of Control," *Journal of Pscyhology and Theology*, 5:4 (1977): 312-17.

393 Courtney, Howard P. *The Vocal Gifts of the Spirit.* B. N. Robertson Company, 1956.

394 Craig, Mary. "The Jesus Movement in Britain," *Catholic Gazette*, 63:9 (1972): 3-7.

395 Crayne, Richard. *Early Twentieth Century Pentecost.* Privately published, n.d.

396 _____. *Pentecostal Handbook.* Privately published, n.d. (c. 1963).

397 Crehan, Joseph. "Charismatics and Pentecostals," *Christian Order*, 13 (October-November 1972): 582-93, 678-89.

398 Cremer, A. H. "Charismata," in *The New Schaff-Herzog Encyclopedia of Religious Knowledge*, S. M. Jackson, editor. 13 vols. Baker Book House, 1950. 3:11.

399 Criswell, W. A. *The Baptism, Filling and Gifts of the Holy Spirit.* Zondervan, 1973.

400 Crocket, Horace L. *Conversations on the Tongues.* Pentecostal Publishing Company, 1929.

401 Culpepper, Robert H. *Evaluating the Charismatic Movement.* The Judson Press, 1977.

402 _____. "Survey of Some Tensions Emerging in the Charismatic Movement," *Scottish Journal of Theology*, 30:5 (1977): 439-52.

403 Cunningham, Raymond J. "From Holiness to Healing: The Faith Cure in America, 1872-1892," *Church History*, 43 (December 1974): 499-513.

404 Currie, Stuart D. "Speaking in Tongues: Early Evidence Outside the New Testament Bearing on 'Glōssais Lalein,' " *Interpretation*, 19 (1965): 274-94.

405 Custeau, J. and R. Michael. *Reconnaître l'Esprit.* Privately published, 1974.

406 Cutten, George B. *The Psychological Phenomena of Christianity.* Scribner's Sons, 1909.

407 _____. *Speaking with Tongues: Historically and Psychologically Considered.* Yale University Press, 1927.

D

408 Daecke, Sigurd Martin. "Für und Wider die Jesus People Bewegung," *Evangelische Kommentare*, 5 (1972): 155-58.

409 Dallièré, Louis. *D'aplomb sur la parole de Dieu. Courte étude sur le Réveil de Pentecôte*. Imprimerie Charpin et Reyne, 1932.

410 Dallmeyer, Heinrich. *Die Zungenbewegung. Ein Beitrag zu ihrer Geschichte und eine Kennzeichnung ihres Geistes*. Buchhandlung der Landeskirchlichen Gemeinschaft, 1924.

411 Dalton, Robert Chandler. "Glossolalia." Unpublished bachelor's thesis, Eastern Baptist Theological Seminary, 1940.

412 _____. *Tongues Like As of Fire*. Gospel Publishing House, 1945.

413 Damboriena, Prudencio. "Pentecostal Fury," *Catholic World*, 202 (January 1966): 217-23.

414 _____. "The Pentecostals In Chile," *Catholic Mind*, 60 (March 1962): 27-32.

415 _____. *Tongues As of Fire: Pentecostalism in Contemporary Christianity*. Corpus Books, 1969.

416 Dana, H. E. *The Holy Spirit in Acts*. Central Seminary Press, 1943.

417 Danielson, D. "A Community of Pentecostals," *Sisters Today*, 43 (December 1971): 215-24.

418 Daugherty, Bob. *New Testament Teaching on Tongues*. Privately published, n.d.

419 Daughtry, Herbert. "A Theology of Black Liberation from a Pentecostal Perspective," *Spirit*, 3:2 (1979): 6-19.

420 Davies, Douglas. "Social Groups, Liturgy, and Glossolalia," *Churchman*, 90 (July-September 1976): 193-205.

421 Davies, Horton. *Christian Deviations: The Challenge of the New Spiritual Movements*. Westminster Press, 1965.

422 _____. "Pentecostalism: Threat or Promise?" *Expository Times*, 76 (March 1965): 197-99.

423 Davies, J. G. "Pentecost and Glossolalia," *Journal of Theological Studies*, 3 (October 1952): 228-31.

424 Davies, J. Hywell. *The Renewal of the Church from a Pentecostal Viewpoint*. World Council of Churches, 1966.

425 Davies, John M. *Pentecost and Today: Tongues and Healing*. Walterick Publishing Co., n.d.

426 Davis, A. S. "Pentecostal Movement in Black Christianity," *The Black Church*, 2 (1972): 65-88.

427 Davis, J. Merle. *How the Church Grows in Brazil: A Study of the Economic and Social Basis of the Evangelical Church in Brazil*. International Mission Conference, 1943.

428 Davis, Kenneth. "Anabaptism as a Charismatic Movement," *Mennonite Quarterly Review*, 53:3 (July 1979): 219-34.

429 _____. "The Origins of Anabaptism: Ascetic and Charismatic Elements Exemplifying Continuity and Discontinuity," in *The Origins and Characteristics of Anabaptism*. Marc Lienhard, editor. Privately published, 1977. Pp. 27-41.

430 Davis, Raymond W. "A Story of Integration," in *The Charismatic Movement*. Michael Hamilton, editor. Eerdmans, 1975. Pp. 175-84.

431 Davis, Rex. "Charismatic Renewal: Impressions From a World Survey," *Study Encounter*, 11:4 (1975): 1-13.

432 _____. *Locusts and Wild Honey: The Charismatic Renewal and the Ecumenical Movement*. World Council of Churches, 1978.

433 Davison, Leslie. *Pathway to Power*. Fountain Trust, 1971.

434 Day, Charles L. "Glossolalia in Biblical and Post-Biblical Perspective." Unpublished doctor's dissertation, Golden Gate Seminary, 1971.

435 Day, Edward. "What We Can Learn from the 'Jesus People,' " *Liguorian*, 61:3 (1973): 2-5.

436 Dayton, Donald W. *The American Holiness Movement: A Bibliographical Introduction*. Asbury Theological Seminary, 1971.

437 _____. "Doctrine of the Baptism of the Holy Spirit: Its Emergence and Significance," *Wesleyan Theological Journal*, 13 (Spring 1978): 114-26.

438 _____. "From Christian Perfection to the 'Baptism of the Holy Ghost,' " in *Aspects of Pentecostal-Charismatic Origins*, Vinson Synan, editor. Logos International, 1975. Pp. 39-54.

439 _____. "The Holiness and Pentecostal Churches: Emerging from Cultural Isolation," *Christian Century*, 96 (August 15-22, 1979): 786-92.

440 _____. "Theological Roots of Pentecostalism," *Pneuma*, 2:1 (Spring 1980): 3-21.

441 Dean, Robert L. "Strange Tongues: A Psychologist Studies Glossolalia," *SK&F Psychiatric Reporter*, 14 (May-June 1964): 15-17.

442 Dearman, Marion. "Christ and Conformity: A Study of Pentecostal Values," *Journal for the Scientific Study of Religion*, 13:4 (1974): 437-53.

443 Decker, Ralph Winefield. "The First Christian Pentecost." Unpublished doctor's dissertation, Boston University, 1941.

444 DeVol, Thomas I. "Ecstatic Pentecostal Prayer and Meditation," *Journal of Religion and Health*, 13:4 (1974): 285-88.

445 Dewar, Lindsay. *The Holy Spirit and Modern Thought*. Harper and Brothers, 1959.

446 _____. "The Problem of Pentecost," *Theology*, 9 (1924): 249-59.

447 Dhorme, P. "L'emploi metaphorique des noms de parties du Corps en hébreu et en akkadien," *Revue Biblique*, 30 (1921): 517-40.

448 Diener, W. *Medio Siglo de Testimonio para Cristo*. Imprenta y Editorial Alianza, n.d.

449 Dieter, Melvin E. "Wesleyan-Holiness Aspects of Pentecostal Origins: As Mediated Through the Nineteenth-Century Holiness Revival," in *Aspects of Pentecostal-Charismatic Origins*, Vinson Synan, editor. Logos International, 1975. Pp. 55-80.

450 Dillistone, F. W. "The Biblical Doctrine of the Holy Spirit," *Theology Today*, 3 (January 1947): 486-97.

451 Dillow, Joseph. *Speaking in Tongues*. Zondervan, 1975.

452 "The Diocese of Chicago's Report on Spiritual Speaking," *The Living Church*, 142 (January 1, 1964): 10-11, 18.

453 Dirks, Lee E. "The Pentecostals: Speaking in Other Tongues," in *National Observer News Book: Religion in Action*. The National Observer, 1965. Pp. 168-276.

454 _____. " 'Tongues' and the Historic Churches," *The National Observer* (October 26, 1964): 8.

455 Dixon, Amzi C., ed. *The Holy Spirit in Life and Service: Addresses Delivered Before the Conference on the Ministry of the Holy Spirit, Brooklyn, 1894*. Revell, 1895.

456 _____. *Speaking with Tongues*. Bible Institute Colportage Association, n.d.

457 Dobbie, Flo. *Land Aflame!* Hodder & Stoughton, 1972.

458 Dollar, George W. "Church History and the Tongues Movement," *Bibliotheca Sacra*, 120 (October-December 1963): 316-21.

459 Dominian, J. "Psychological Evaluation of the Pentecostal Movement," *Expository Times*, 87 (July 1976): 292-97.

460 Dominy, Bert. "Paul and Spiritual Gifts: Reflections on 1 Corinthians 12-14," *Southwestern Journal of Theology*, 26:1 (Fall 1983): 49-68.

461 Donovan, John J. "Religious Revivalism as Counter-Culture," *Spiritual Life*, 18:1 (1972): 47-57.

462 Douglas, J. D. "Tongues in Transition," *Christianity Today*, 10 (July 8, 1966): 34.

463 Doutreloux, Albert and Colette Degive. "Perspective Anthropologique sur un mouvement Religieux Actuel," *Social Compass*, 25:1 (1978): 43-54.

464 Dowden, Milton L. "Why Did Paul Rebaptize the Twelve Disciples in Acts 19:1-7." Unpublished report, Grace Theological Seminary, 1950.

465 Drummond, Andrew L. *Edward Irving and His Cicle*. Privately published,1937.

466 Duchesne, Jean. *Jesus Revolution Made in USA*. Fontanella, 1972.

467 Duewel, Wesley L. *The Holy Spirit and Tongues*. Light and Life Press, 1974.

468 Dufort, Jean M. "Comportements et Attitudes dans les Groupes charismatiques: une lecture herméneutique," *Science et Esprit*, 30 (October-December 1978): 255-78.

469 _____. "Emergence du Renouveau charismatique dans les églises chrétiennes," *Science et Esprit*, 30 (May-September 1978): 143-67.

470 _____. "Vues prospectives sur le Renouveau charismatique dans les eglises chrétiennes," *Science et Esprit*, 31 (January-April 1979): 61-79.

471   Dunn, James D. G. *Baptism in the Holy Spirit*. Allenson, 1970.

472   _____. *Baptism in the Holy Spirit: A Re-examination of the New Testament Teaching on the Gift of the Spirit in Relation to Pentecostalism Today*. SCM Press, 1970.

473   _____. "Discernment of Spirits: A Neglected Gift," in *The Witness of the Spirit*, Wilfrid Harrington, editor. Irish Biblical Association, 1979. Pp. 79-96.

474   _____. *Jesus and the Spirit*. SCM Press, 1975.

475   _____. "Rediscovering the Spirit," *Expository Times*, 84 (1972): 7-12, 40-44.

476   _____. "Spirit-Baptism and Pentecostalism," *Scottish Journal of Theology*, 23 (1970): 397-407.

477   _____. "Spirit-and-Fire Baptism," *Novum Testamentum*, 14 (1972): 81-92.

478   DuPlessis, David J. "A Brief History of Pentecostal Movements." Unpublished manuscript, n.d.

479   _____. *Glossolalia*. Privately published, n.d.

480   _____. "Golden Jubilees of Twentieth-Century Pentecostal Movements," *International Review of Mission*, 47:2 (n.d.) 193-201.

481   _____. "The Historic Background of Pentecostalism," *One in Christ*, 10 (1974): 174-79.

482   _____. *The Life of Andrew Murray of South Africa*. Marshall Brothers, 1920.

483   _____. *A Man Called Mr. Pentecost*. Logos International, 1977.

484   _____. *Pentecost Outside "Pentecost."* Privately published, 1960.

485   _____. "A Pentecostal and the Ecumenical Movement," in *What the Spirit is Saying to the Churches*, Theodore Runyon, editor. Hawthorne Books, 1975. Pp. 91-103.

486   _____. *The Spirit Bade Me Go*. Logos International, 1972.

487   Dupont, J. "La première Pentecôte chrétienne," *Assemblées du Seigneurm*, 51 (1963): 39-62.

488   _____. "Le problème des langues dans l'Église de Corinthe," *Proche-Orient Chrétien*, 12 (1962): 3-12.

489   _____. "Le Salut des Gentils et la Signification Théologigue du Livre des Actes," *New Testament Studies*, 6 (January 1960): 132-55.

490 Duquoc, Christian. "Charism as the Social Expression of the Unpredictable Nature of Grace," in *Charisms in the Church,* Christian Duquoc and Casiano Floristan, editors. The Seabury Press, 1978. Pp. 87-96.

491 Duquoc, Christian and Casiano Floristan, eds. *Charisms in the Church.* The Seabury Press, 1978.

492 Durand, Pierre. "Une information sur le mouvement charismatique," *Amitié,* 2 (1973): 31-33.

493 Durasoff, Steve. "The All-Union Council of Evangelical Christians-Baptists in the Soviet Union: 1944-1964." Unpublished doctor's dissertation, New York University, 1967.

494 _____. "An Abstract of the All-Union Council of Evangelical Christians—Baptists in the Soviet Union: 1944-1964." Unpublished paper, 1967.

495 _____. *Bright Wind of the Spirit: Pentecostalism Today.* Prentice-Hall, 1973.

496 _____. The Russian Protestants: Evangelicals in the Soviet Union, 1944-1964. Fairleigh Dickenson University Press, 1971.

497 Dussel, Enrique. "The Differentiation of Charisms," in *Charisms in the Church,* Christian Duquoc and Casiano Floristan, editors. The Seabury Press, 1978. Pp. 38-55.

498 Dye, M. L. *The Murderous Communist Conspiracy: Satan's End-Time Program.* Anchor Bay Evangelistic Association, n.d.

499 Dyer, Luther B. *Tongues.* LeRoi Publishers, 1971.

500 Dynes, Russell R. "Church-Sect Typology and Socio-Economic Status," *American Sociological Review,* 20 (1955): 555-60.

E

501 Eason, Gerald M. "The Significance of Tongues." Unpublished master's thesis, Dallas Theological Seminary, 1959.

502 Eastman, Dick. *Up with Jesus*. Baker Book House, 1971.

503 Easton, Burton Scott. "Tongues, Confusion of," in *The International Standard Bible Encyclopedia*. 5 vols. The Howard-Severance Company, 1915. 5: 2994-95.

504 ————. "Tongues, Gift of," in *The International Standard Bible Encyclopedia*. 5 vols. The Howard-Severance Company, 1915. 5: 2995-97.

505 Ecke, Karl. *Die Pfingstbewegung. Ein Gutachten von kirchlicher Siete*. Christl. Gemeinschaftsverband GmbH, 1950.

506 Edel, Eugene. *Der Kampf um die Pfingstbewegung*. Privately published, 1949.

507 Edel, Reiner-Friedemann, ed. *Die Bedeutung der Gnadengaben für die Femeinde Jesus Christi*. (Oekumenische Texte und Studien 33). Edel, 1964.

508 ————. *Im Fraftfeld des Heiligen Geistes*. Edel, 1968.

509 ————. *Kirche und Charisma. Die Gaben des Heiligen Geistes im Neuen Testament, in der Kirchengeschichte und in der Gegenwart*. Edel, 1966.

510 Edman, Raymond V. "Divine or Devilish?" *Christian Herald*, 87 (May 1964): 14-17.

511 Edwards, Hubert E. "The Tongues at Pentecost: A Suggestion," *Theology*, 16 (1928): 248-52.

512 Edwards, O. C. "The Exegesis of Acts 8:4-25 and Its Implications for Confirmation and Glossolalia," *Anglican Theological Review*, supplementary series, 2 (September 1973): 100-12.

513 Eggenberger, Oswald. "Zur Auswirkung der Jesus-Bewegung in der Schweiz," *Kirchenblatt für die reformierte Schweiz*, 128 (1972): 258-61, 275-78.

514 _____. *Evangelischer Glaube und Pfingstbewegung*. Evangelischer Verlag, 1956.

515 _____. "Die Geistestaufe in der gegenwärtigen Pfingstbewegung," *Theologische Zeitschrift*, 11 (Jully-August 1955): 272-95.

516 _____. "Die neue Zungenbeweung in Amerika," *Theologische Zeitschrift*, 21 (September-October 1965): 427-46.

517 Ehrenstein, Herbert Henry. "Glosslalia: First Century and Today," *The King's Business*, (November 1964): 31-34.

518 Ehrhardt, Arnold. "The Construction and Purpose of the Acts of the Apostles," *Studia Theologica*, 12 (1958): 45-79.

519 Eicherl, Margrit. "Charismatic Prophets and Charismatic Saviours (Munster Anabaptists and Jan Van Leyden)," *Mennonite Quarterly Review*, 55 (January 1981): 45-61.

520 Eicken, Erich von. *Heiliger Geist, Menschengeist, Schwarmgeist. Ein Beitrag zur Geschichte der Pfingstbewegung in Deutschland*. R. Brockhaus-Verlag, 1964.

521 Eimer, Robert. "The Catholic Pentecostal Movement," *The Priest*, 27:3 (March 1971): 335-43.

522 Eisenlöffel, Ludwig. "Die Erneuerung der Kirche aus der Sicht der Pfingstbewegung," *Der Leuchter*, 17:2 (November 1966): 5-7.

523 _____. *Ein Feuer auf Erden. Einführung in Lehre und Leben der Pfingstbewegung*. Leuchter-Verlag, 1963.

524 Eliade, Mircea. *Le chamanisme et les techniques archaïques de l'extase*. Privately published, 1951.

525 _____. *Myths, Dreams and Mysteries*. Harper and Row, 1960.

526 _____. *Shamanism: Archaic Techniques of Ecstasy*. Trans. by Willard R. Trask. Pantheon Books, 1964.

527 Elinson, Howard. "The Implications of Pentecostal Religion for Intellectualism, Politics and Race Relations," *American Journal of Sociology*, 70 (1965): 403-15.

528 Ellis, E. Earle. " 'Spiritual Gifts' in the Pauline Community," *New Testament Studies*, 10 (1974): 128-44.

529 Ellis, Paul N. "Concerning 'Tongues,' " *Light and Life*, (June 1972): 9.

530 Ellis, William T. "Have Gift of Tongues," *Chicago Daily News*, (January 14, 1908): 10.

531 Ellison, Jerome. *God on Broadway*. John Knox Press, 1971.

532 Ellison, Robert W. "Charismatic Renewal and Practical Usage," *Dialog*, 13:1 (1974): 33-39.

533 Elsom, John R. *Pentecostalism Versus the Bible: or, The Tongues Movement and Why I Left It*. Wetzel Publishing Company, 1937.

534 Emmert, Athanasios F.S. "Charismatic Developments in the Eastern Orthodox Church," in *Perspectives on the New Pentecostalism*, Russell Spittler, editor. Baker Book House, 1976. Pp. 28-42.

535 Engelsen, Nils Ivar Johan. "Glossolalia and Other Forms of Inspired Speech According to 1 Corinthians 12-14." Unpublished doctor's dissertation, Yale, 1970.

536 _____. "Glossolalia and Other Forms of Inspired Speech According to 1 Corinthians 12-14," *Parole di Vita*, 6 (1971): 376-87.

537 Engelsviken, Tormod. "The Gift of the Spirit: An Analysis and Evaluation of the Charismatic Movement from a Lutheran Theological Perspective." Unpublished doctor's dissertation, Acquinas Institute, 1981.

538 _____. *Den Hellige ands 1 Kirkkens Liv*. Luther Forlag, 1981. 1981.

539 _____. "Molo Wongel: A Documentary Report on the Life and History of the Independent Pentecostal Movement in Ethiopia 1960-1975." Typescript manuscript. Oslo, 1975.

540 Engelsviken, Tormod, Hanssen Ove, and Sannes Kjell, eds. *Den Hellige ands 1 Kirkkens Liv*. Luther Forlag, 1981.

541 Ennis, Philip H. "Ecstasy and Everyday Life," *Journal for the Scientific Study of Religion*, 6 (1967): 40-48.

542 Enroth, Ronald M., Edward E. Ericson and C. Breckenridge Peters. *The Jesus People: Old-Time Religion in the Age of Aquarius*. Eerdmans, 1972.

543 Ensley, Eddie. *Sounds of Wonder: Speaking in Tongues in the Catholic Tradition*. Paulist Press, 1977.

544 Epp, Theodore H. *Gifts of the Spirit*. Back to Bible Publications, 1954.

545 Epp, Theodore H. and John I Paton. "The Use and Abuse of Tongues." A sermon, Back to the Bible Broadcast, Lincoln, Nebraska, 1963.

546 Erasmus, D. J. "Enkele Gedagtes oor Glossolalie," *Nederlands Theologisch Tijdschrift*, 12 (April 1971): 247-61.

547 Erickson, E. C. *The Bible on Speaking in Tongues*. Privately published, n.d.

548 Ervin, Howard M. *And Fobid Not to Speak With Tongues*. Logos International, n.d.

549 _____. "As the Spirit Gives Utterance," *Christianity Today*, 13 (April 11, 1969): 7-8, 10.

550 _____. "Hermeneutics: A Pentecostal Option," *Pneuma*, 3:2 (Fall 1981): 11-25.

551 _____. *These are Not Drunken, as You Suppose*. Logos International, 1968.

552 Estes, Joseph Richard. "The Biblical Concept of Spiritual Gifts." Unpublished doctor's dissertation, Southern Baptist Theological Seminary, 1957.

553 Eugène de Villeurbanne, O.F.M. Un Fau renouveau: Le pentecôtisme dit "catholique." Bellarmin, 1976.

554 Evans, Leonard H. "A Witness," *Charisma Digest*, 2 (1969): 11-13, 27-33.

555 Ewald, Tod W. "Aspects of Tongues," *The Living Church*, 146 (June 2, 1963): 12-13, 19.

556 _____. "Aspects of Tongues," *View*, 2:1 (1965): 7-11.

557 Ewart, Frank J. *The Phenomenon of Pentecost: A History of the Latter Rain*. Pentecostal Publishing House, 1947.

558 Ewin, Wilson. "Key 73 and Roman Catholic Pentecostal (Charismatic) Power," *Reformation Review*, 20 (1973): 227-43.

F

559 Failing, George E. "Should I Speak with Tongues," *The Wesleyan Methodist*, 122 (January 20, 1965): 6.

560 Failing, Wolf-Eckart. "Neue charismatische Bewegung in den Landeskirchen," in *Pfingstkirchen*, W. J. Hollenweger, editor. Evangelische Verlagswerk, 1971. Pp. 131-45.

561 Falconi, Carlo. *LaChiesa e le organizzazioni cattoliche in Italia, 1945-1955. Saggi per una storia del cattolicesimo italiano ne dopoguerra*. Privately published, 1956.

562 "The Famous Oracle at Delphi," *National Geographic Magazine*, 85 (March 1944): 304-305.

563 Farah, Charles. "A Critical Analysis: The 'Roots and Fruits' of Faith-Formula Theology," *Pneuma*, 3:1 (Spring 1981): 3-21.

564 Farrell, Frank. "Outburst of Tongues: The New Penetration," *Christianity Today*, 7 (September 13, 1963): 3-7.

565 "Fastest-Growing Church in the Hemisphere," *Time*, 80 (November 2, 1962): 56.

566 Faupel, David W. *The American Pentecostal Movement: A Bibliographic Essay*. Asbury Theological Library, 1972.

567 _____. "The Function of 'Models' in the Interpretation of Pentecostal Thought," *Pneuma*, 2:1 (Spring 1980): 51-71.

568 Fee, Gordon D. "Hermeneutics and Historical Precedent: A Major Problem in Pentecostal Hermeneutics" in *Perspectives on the New Pentecostalism*, Russell F. Spittler, editor. Baker Book House, 1976. Pp. 118-32.

569 _____. "Tongues: Least of the Gifts: Some Exegetical Observations on 1 Corinthians 12-14," *Pneuma*, 2:2 (Fall 1980): 3-14.

570 Feine, Paul. "Speaking with Tongues," *The New Schaff-Herzog Encyclopedia of Religious Knowledge*, S. M. Jackson, editor. 15 vols. Baker Book House, 1950. 11: 36-39.

571 _____. "Zungenreden," in *Realencyklopädie für protestantische Theologie und Kirch*. 24 vols. J. C. Hinrichs, 1908. 21: 749-59.

572 Ferguson, Charles W. *The Confusion of Tongues: A Review of Modern Isms*. Doubleday, Doran and Company, 1928.

573 Fernández del Rio, P. "Hablar en lenguas: Precedentes histórico-literários e interpretación exegética en el Nuevo Testamento." Unpublished dissertation, Pontifical Biblical Institute, 1973.

574 Fernandez, Pedro. "El neopentecostalismo catolico una evaluacion teologica," *Dialogo Ecumenico*, 8 (1973): 395-445.

575 Ferry, Anthony. "Oh, Sing It, You Precious Pentecostal People!" *Macleans*, 85 (November 3, 1962): 20-23.

576 Fichter, Joseph H. *The Catholic Cult of the Paraclete*. Sheed and Word, 1973.

577 _____. "Liberal and Conservative Catholic Pentecostals," *Social Compass*, 21 (1974): 303-10.

578 _____. "Parallel Conversions: Charismatics and Recovered Alcoholics," *Christian Century*, 93 (February 18, 1976): 148-50.

579 _____. "Pentecostals: Comfort vs. Awareness," *America*, 129:5 (September 1, 1973): 114-16.

580 Fidler, R. L. "Historical Review of the Pentecostal Outpouring in Los Angeles at the Azusa Street Mission in 1906," *The International Outlook*, (January-March 1963): 3-14.

581 Finch, John G. "God-Inspired or Self-Induced," *Christian Herald*, 87 (May 1964): 12-13, 17, 19.

582 Fink, Paul R. "The Phenomenon of Tongues as Presented in Scripture." Unpublished research paper, Dallas Theological Seminary, 1960.

583 Finney, Charles Grandison. *Lectures on Systematic Theology*. Oberlin College, 1846.

584 Fiorentino, Joseph. *The New Pentecost and the Old*. Privately published, 1971.

585 Fischer, B. "The Meaning of the Expression 'Baptism of the Spirit' in the Light of Catholic Baptismal Liturgy and Spirituality," *One in Christ*, 10 (1974): 172-73.

586 Fischer, Harold A. "Progress of the Various Modern Pentecostal Movements Toward World Fellowship." Unpublished master's thesis, Texas Christian University, 1952.

587 Fisher, J. Franklin. *Speaking with Tongues*. Privately published, n.d.

588 Fishman, Joshua A. "Some Contrasts Between Linguistically Homogeneous and Linguistically Heterogeneous Politics," in *Explorations in Sociolinguistics*, Stanley Liberson, editor. Mouton and Company, 1966. Pp. 18-30.

589 Fisk, Samuel. *Speaking in Tongues in the Light of the Scripture*. College Press, 1972.

590 Fison, J. E. *The Blessing of the Holy Spirit*. Longmans, Green, and Company, 1950.

591 Fleisch, D. Paul. *Zur Geschichte der Heiligungsbewegung*, I. Heft: *Die Heiligungsbewegung von Wesley bis Boardman*. Feesche Verlag, 1910.

592 _____. *Die Pfingstbewegung in Deutschland*. Feesche Verlag, 1957.

593 Fletcher, William C. "American Influence on Russian Religion: The Case of the Pentecostals," *Journal of Church and State*, 20 (Spring 1978): 215-32.

594 Flora, C. B. "Social Dislocation and Pentecostalism: A Multivariate Analysis," *Sociological Analysis*, 34 (Winter 1973): 296-304.

595 Flournoy, Theodore. *From India to the Planet Mars: A Study of a Case of Somnambulism with Glossolalia*. Trans. Daniel B. Vermilye. Harper and Brothers, 1900.

596 Flynn, Thomas. *The Charismatic Renewal and the Irish Experience*. Hodder & Stoughton, 1974.

597 "Foi et vie," *Renouveau charismatique*, 4:5 (July-October 1973): 72.

598 Forbes, James A. "A Pentecostal Approach to Empowerment for Black Liberation." Unpublished doctor's dissertation, Colgate Rochester Divinity School, 1975.

599 Ford, Clay. *Berkeley Journal: Jesus and the Street People—A Firsthand Report*. Harper and Brothers, 1972.

600 Ford, J. Massyngberde. *Baptism of the Spirit: Three Essays on the Pentecostal Experience*. Divine Word Publications, 1971.

601 _____. "Catholic Pentecostalism: New Testament Christianity or Twentieth-Century Hysteria?" *Jubilee*, 16 (June 1968): 13-17.

602 ————. "Catholicisme pentecôtiste," *Concilium*, 79 (1972): 83-87.

603 ————. "The Catholic Charismatic Gifts in Worship," in *The Charismatic Movement*, Michael Hamilton, editor. Eerdmans, 1975. Pp. 114-23.

604 ————. *Ministries and Fruits of the Holy Spirit*. Catholic Action Office, 1973.

605 ————. "Neo-Pentecostalism Within the Roman Catholic Communion," *Dialog*, 13:1 (1974): 45-50.

606 ————. "The New Pentecostalism: Personal Reflections of a Participating Roman Catholic Scholar," in *Perspectives on the New Pentecostalism*, Russell F. Spittler, editor. Baker Book House, 1976. Pp. 108-29.

607 ————. "Pentecostal Catholicism," *Concilium*, 79 (1972): 85-90.

608 ————. *The Pentecostal Experience: A New Direction for American Catholics*. Paulist Press, 1970.

609 ————. "Pentecostal Poise or Docetic Charismatics?" *Spiritual Life*, 19 (1973): 32-47.

610 ————. *The Spirit and the Human Person: A Meditation*. Pflaum Press, 1969.

611 ————. "Spontaneous Prayer Groups," *Sisters Today*, 46 (February 1970): 342-47.

612 ————. "The Theology of Tongues in Relationship to the Individual," *Bible Today*, 8 (April 1970): 3314-20.

613 ————. "Tongues-Leadership-Women: Further Reflections on the New-Pentecostal Movement," *Spiritual Life*, 17 (Fall 1971): 186-97.

614 ————. "Toward a Theology of 'Speaking in Tongues,' " *Theological Studies*, 32 (1971): 3-29.

615 ————. *Which Way for Catholic Pentecostals*. Harper and Row, 1976.

616 Ford, John T. "Tongues, Gift of," in *The Encyclopedia Americana*. 30 vols. Americana Corporation, 1971. 26: 839.

617 Forest, Tom. "Tongues: A Gift of Roses," *New Covenant*, 11:1 (July 1981): 15-17.

618 Forster, Greg S. "The Third Arm: Pentecostal Christianity," *T. S. F. Bulletin*, 63 (1972): 5-9; 64 (1972): 16-21.

619 Foster, Fred J. *Think It Not Strange: A History of the Oneness Movement*. Pentecostal Publishing House, 1965.

620 Foster, Kenneth N. *I Believe in Tongues, but—*. Victory Press, 1976.

621 Fowler, J. Russell. "Holiness, the Spirit's Infilling, and Speaking with Tongues," *Paraclete*, 2 (Summer 1968): 7-9.

622 Fraikin, Daniel. " 'Charismes et Mivisteres' as la Lumiere de 1 Corinthians 12-14," *Eglise et Theologie*, 8:3 (1978): 455-63.

623 Frame, Raymond. "Something Unusual," *His*, 24 (December 1963): 18-30.

624 Francis, Dale. "The Pentecostal Movement and Catholics," *Twin Circle*, 2 (July 29, 1965): 6.

625 Fraser, Maria M. *The Deplorable State of Pentecostal Movements in South Africa*. The Latter Rain Assemblies of South Africa, 1957.

626 Freund, Julien. "Charisme Selon Max Weber," *Social Compass*, 23:4 (1976): 383-95.

627 Friedman, F. G. "Die Jesus People in den Vereinigten Straaten von Amerika," *Internationale Katholische Zeitschrift*, 3 (May-June 1973): 193-205.

628 Frodsham, Stanley. *The Life of Joy*. Gospel Publishing House, n.d.

629 _____. *Smith Wigglesworth: Apostle of Faith*. Gospel Publishing House, 1949.

630 _____. *The Spirit-Filled Life*. Eerdmans, 1948.

631 _____. *With Signs Following: The Story of the Pentecostal Revival in the Twentieth Century*. Gospel Publishing House, 1946.

632 _____. *Wholly for God*. Gospel Publishing House, n.d.

633 Froelich, Karlfried. "Charismatic Manifestations and the Lutheran Incarnational Stance," in *The Holy Spirit in the Life of the Church: From Biblical Times to the Present*, Paul D. Opsahl, editor. Augsburg Publishing House, 1978. Pp. 136-57.

634 Frøen, Hans J. "What is Baptism in the Holy Spirit?" in *Jesus, Where are You Taking Us?* Norris Wogen, editor. Creation House, 1973. Pp. 24-36.

635 Frost, Robert C. *Aglow with the Spirit*. Voice Christian Publications, 1965.

636 Fry, C. George. "Pentecostalism in Historical Perspective," *The Springfielder*, 39 (March 1976): 183-93.

637 —————. "Survey of Protestant and Roman Catholic Confessional Statements in the Twentieth Century," *Concordia Theological Quarterly*, 42 (July 1978): 276-304.

638 Fuller, Reginald H. "Tongues in the New Testament," *American Church Quarterly*, 3 (Fall 1963): 162-68.

639 Fung, Ronald Y. K. "Charismatic versus Organized Ministry: An Examination of an Alleged Antithesis," *Evangelical Quarterly*, 52 (October-December 1980): 195-214.

G

640 Gaddis, Merle E. "Christian Perfectionism in America." Unpublished doctor's dissertation, University of Chicago, 1928.

641 Gaebelein, A. C. and F. C. Jennings. *Pentecostalism, the Gift of Tongues and Demon Possession*. Our Hope Publication Office, n.d.

642 _____. "The So-Called Gift of Tongues," *Our Hope*, 14 (July 1907): 13-16.

643 Gaëte, Arturo. "Un cas d'adaptation: Les 'Pentecostales' au Chili," in *L'Eglise, l'occident, le monde*, R. P. Abd-el-Jali, Daniel Rops, R. P. Houang, Olivier Lacombe, Pierre-Henry Simon, editors. Arthème Fayard, 1956. Pp. 142-49.

644 Galanter, Macc. "Charismatic Religious Sects and Psychiatry: An Overview," *American Journal of Psychiatry*, 139:12 (1982): 1539-48.

645 Gangel, Kenneth O. *You and Your Spiritual Gifts*. Moody Press, 1975.

646 Ganoczy, Alexandre. "Word and Spirit in the Catholic Tradition," in *Conflicts About the Holy Spirit*, Hans Küng and Jürgen Moltmann, editors. The Seabury Press, 1979. Pp. 48-59.

647 Gardiner, James J. and J. D. Roberts. *Quest for a Black Theology*. Pilgrim Press, 1972.

648 Garrigues, J. M. "L'effusion de l'Esprit," *Vie spirituelle*, 128 (1974): 73-81.

649 Gause, R. Hollis. "Issues in Pentecostalism," in *Perspectives on the New Pentecostalism*, Russell F. Spittler, editor. Baker Book House, 1976. Pp. 106-16.

650 Gaver, Jessyca. *Pentecostalism*. Award Book, 1971.

651 Gee, Donald. *All With One Accord*. Gospel Publishing House, 1961.

652 _____. *Concerning Spiritual Gifts*. Gospel Publishing House, 1947.

653 _____. "Critics and Criticism," *Pentecost*, 35 (March 1965): 17.

654 _____. "Do 'Tongues' Matter?" *Pentecost*, 49 (September 1958): 17.

655 _____. "Don't Spill the Wine," *Pentecost*, 61 (September-November 1962): 17.

656 _____. *The Fruit of the Spirit*. Gospel Publishing House, 1934.

657 _____. *Fruitful or Barren: Studies in the Fruit of the Spirit*. Gospel Publishing House, 1961.

658 _____. *God's Great Gift*. The Gospel Publishing House, n.d.

659 _____. "The Initial Evidence of the Baptism of the Holy Spirit," *Redemption Tidings*, 45 (1959): 10-12.

660 _____. *Keeping in Touch: Studies on "Walking in the Spirit."* Elim Publishing Company, 1951.

661 _____. *The Ministry Gifts of Christ*. Gospel Publishing House, 1930.

662 _____. "Movement Without a Man," *Christian Life*, 28 (July 1966): 52.

663 _____. *Pentecost*. 34 (December 1955): 10.

664 _____. *The Pentecostal Movement*. Elim Publishing Company, 1949.

665 _____, ed. "Pentecostal World Conference Messages." Preached at the Fifth Triennial World Conference held in Toronto, Canada. Published by the Advisory Committee for the Conference. Testimony Press, 1958.

666 _____. "The Phenomena of Pentecost," in *The Phenomena of Pentecost*, D. Gee, P. C. Nelson, Myer Pearlman, George Jeffreys, D. W. Kerr, editors. Gospel Publishing House, 1931. Pp. 5-13.

667 _____. *Proverbs for Pentecost*. Gospel Publishing House, 1936.

668 _____. *Story of a Great Revival*. Gospel Publishing House, n.d.

669 _____. *This is the Will of God*. Elim Publishing Company, 1940.

670 _____. "To the Uttermost Part: The Missionary Results of the
    Pentecostal Movement in the British Isles," *Redemption Tidings*,
    (n.d.).

671 _____. *Toward Pentecostal Unity*. Gospel Publishing House,
    n.d.

672 _____. *Upon All Flesh*. Gospel Publishing House, 1935; The
    Gospel Publishing House, 1947.

673 _____. "Wheat, Tares and 'Tongues.' " *Pentecost*, 67 (December 1963-February 1964): 17.

674 _____. *Why "Pentecost?"* Privately published, 1944.

675 _____. "Why Is 'Pentecost' Opposed?" *Pentecostal Testimony*,
    10 (November 1929): 16.

676 Gee, Donald, J. N. Gartner and H. Pickering. *Water Baptism and the
    Trinity*. Gospel Publishing House, n.d.

677 Gelpi, Donald L. "American Pentecostalism," *Spiritual Revivals*,
    C. Duquoc and C. Floristán, editors. Herder and Herder, 1973.
    Pp. 101-10.

678 _____. *Charisma and Sacrament*. Paulist Press, 1976; SPCK,
    1977.

679 _____. "Conversion: The Challenge of Contemporary Charismatic Piety," *Theological Studies*, 43 (December 1982): 606-28.

680 _____. *Experiencing God: A Theology of Human Experience*.
    Paulist Press, 1978.

681 _____. "Pentecostal Theology: A Roman Catholic Viewpoint,"
    in *Perspectives on the New Pentecostalism*, Russell F. Spittler,
    editor. Baker Book House, 1976. Pp. 86-103.

682 _____. *Pentecostalism: A Theological Viewpoint*. Paulist
    Press, 1971.

683 _____. "Le pentecôtisme américain," *Concilium*, 89 (1973):
    91-99.

684 _____. "Understanding Spirit-Baptism: As Catholic Pentecostals Practice It," *America*, 122 (May 16, 1970): 520-21.

685 "Gemeinde für Urchristentum." *Wer wir sind*. Oberhofen, n.d.

686 "Gemeinde Jesus Christ." *Wer ist die Gemeinde Jesu Christi in
    Deutschland?* Stammheim, n.d.

687 George, Martin. *Scripture and the Charismatic Renewal*. Servant
    Books, 1979.

688 Geppert, Hans Jürgen. *Wir Gotteskinder: Die Jesus-People Bewegung.* J. C. B. Mohr, 1972.

689 Gerest, Claude. "The Hour of Charisms: The Development of the Charismatic Movements in America," in *Charisms in the Church*, Christian Duquoc and Casiano Floristan, editors. The Seabury Press, 1978. Pp. 13-37.

690 _____. "Mouvements spirituels et institutions écclésiales," *Concilium*, 89 (1973): 35-50.

691 Gericke, P. *Christliche Vollkommenheit und Geisteserlebnisse.* Privately published, 1950.

692 Gerlach, Joel C. "Glossolalia," *Wisconsin Lutheran Quarterly* (October 1973): 251.

693 Gerlach, Luther P. "Pentecostalism: Revolution or Counter-Revolution?" in *Religious Movements in Contemporary America*, Irving I. Zaretsky and Mark P. Leone, editors. Princeton University Press, 1974. Pp. 669-99.

694 _____. *People, Power, Change: Movements of Social Transformation.* Bobbs-Merrill, 1970.

695 Gerlach, Luther P. and Virginia H. Hine. "The Charismatic Revival: Process and Recruitment, Conversion, and Behavior Change in Modern Religious Movements." Unpublished paper, University of Minnesota, 1966.

696 _____. "Five Factors Crucial to the Growth and Spread of a Modern Religious Movement," *Journal for the Scientific Study of Religion*, 7 (1968): 23-40.

697 Gerrard, Nathan Lewis. "The Holiness Movement in Southern Appalachia," in *The Charismatic Movement*, Michael Hamilton, editor. Eerdmans, 1975. Pp. 159-71.

698 _____. "The Serpent-Handling Religions of West Virginia," *Transaction*, (May 1968): 22-30.

699 Gewiess, J. "Glossolalie," *Lexikon für Theologie und Kirche*, 4 (1960): 972-73.

700 Giblet, J. "Baptism in the Spirit in the Acts of the Apostles," *One in Christ*, 10 (1974): 162-71.

701 _____. "Le mouvement pentecôtiste dans l'eglise catholique des U.S.A.," *Review théologique de Louvain*, 4 (1973): 469-90.

702 "The Gift of Tongues," *The Perspective Review*, 8 (1852): 303-17.

703 Gijs, Jan van. *Het feest gaat door!* Kracht van Omhoog, 1962.

704 Gilbert, Arthur. "Pentecost Among the Pentecostals," *Christian Century*, 78 (June 28, 1961): 794-96.

705 Gill, Merton and Margaret Brenman. *Hypnosis and Related States: Psychoanalytic Studies in Regression*. International Universities Press, 1959.

706 Gillespie, T. W. "Pattern of Prophetic Speech in 1 Corinthians," *Journal of Biblical Literature*, 97 (March 1978): 74-95.

707 _____. "Prophecy and Tongues." Unpublished dissertation, Claremont Graduate School and University Center, 1971.

708 Gilmore, Susan K. "Personality Differences Between High and Low Dogmatism Groups of Pentecostal Believers," *Journal for the Scientific Study of Religion*, 8 (1969): 161-64.

709 Gilmour, S. MacLean. "Easter and Pentecost," *Journal of Biblical Literature*, 81 (March 1962): 62-66.

710 Glardon, Christian. "Les dons spirituels dans la première épître de Paul aux Corinthians." Thèse, présentée à la Faculté de Thèologie de l'Eglise évangélique libre du Canton de Vaud pour obtenir le grade de licencié en théologie, Lausanne, University, 1966.

711 Glazier, Stephen D. *Perspectives on Pentecostalism: Case Studies from the Caribbean and Latin America*, University Press of America, 1980.

712 "Glossolalia," *The Living Church*, 146 (May 19, 1963): 11-12.

713 "Glossolalia," in *The Oxford Dictionary of the Christian Church*, F. L. Cross, editor. Oxford University Press, 1958. P. 564.

714 Glover, John. "Summary Analysis and Conclusions," in *Tongues*, Luther B. Dyer, editor. LeRoi Publishers, 1971. Pp. 142-51.

715 Glynne, W. "Psychology and Glossolalia: The Book of Acts," *Church Quarterly Review*, 106 (July 1928): 281-300.

716 Godin, André. "Moi Perdu on Moi Retrouvé daas l'expérience Charismatique," *Archives de Sciences Sociales des Religions*, 20 (July-December 1975): 31-52.

717 Goettmann, J. "La Pentecôte premices de la nouvelle création," *Bible et vie chrétienne*, 27 (1959): 59-69.

718 Goforth, Jonathan. *By My Spirit*. Zondervan, 1942.

719 Goldingax, John. *The Church and the Gifts of the Spirit: A Practical Exposition of 1 Corinthians 12-14*. Grove Books, 1972.

720 Goldsmith, Henry. "The Psychological Usefulness of Glossolalia to the Believer," *View*, 2 (November 2, 1965): 7-8.

721 Gonsalvez, Emma. "A Psychological Interpretation of the Religious Behavior of Pentecostals and Charismatics," *Journal of Dharma*, 7 (October-December 1982): 408-29.

722 —————. "The Theology and Psychology of Glossolalia." Doctoral dissertation, Northwestern University, 1978.

723 Goodman, Felicitas D. "The Acquisition of Glossolalia Behavior," *Semiotica*, 3 (1971): 77-82.

724 —————. "Altered Mental States vs. 'Style of Discourse': Reply to Samarin," *Journal for the Scientific Study of Religion*, 11 (1972): 197-99.

725 —————. "Disturbances in the Apostolic Church: Case Study of a Trance-Based Upheaval in Yucatan." Unpublished doctor's dissertation, Ohio State University, 1971.

726 —————. "Glossolalia and Hallucination in Pentecostal Congregations." Paper presented to the annual meeting of the American Anthropological Association, New York, 1971.

727 —————. "Glossolalia and Single-Limb Trance: Some Parallels," *Psychotherapy and Psychosomatics*, 19 (1971): 92-103.

728 —————. "Phonetic Analysis of Glossolalia in Four Cultural Settings," *Journal for the Scientific Study of Religion*, 8 (1969): 227-39.

729 —————. *Speaking in Tongues: A Cross-Cultural Study of Glossolalia*. University of Chicago Press, 1972.

730 —————, et al. *Trance, Healing and Hallucination*. John Wiley & Sons, 1974.

731 Goodwin, John W. *The Miracle of Pentecost: or, The Evidence by Speaking in Tongues*. Nazarene Publishing House, n.d.

732 Gordon, A. J. *The Ministry of the Spirit*. Revell, 1894.

733 Gosnell, L. W. "The Gift of Tongues: The True and the False," *The Christian Workers Magazine*, 13 (November 1913): 1-11.

734 Goss, Ethel E., ed. *The Winds of God : The Story of the Early Pentecostal Days (1901-1914) in the Life of Howard Goss*. Comet Press, 1958.

735 Gouvernaire, J. "Les charismatiques," *Études* 340 (January-June 1974): 123-40.

736 "Government and Glossolalia," *Christianity Today*, 8 (July 31, 1964): 44-45.

737 "Government Grant for Study of 'Speaking in Tongues,' " *Pastoral Psychology*, 15 (September 1964): 53-54.

738 Graham, Billy. *The Jesus Generation*. Hodder & Stoughton, 1972.

739 _____. "Something is Happening," in *The Baptists and the Baptism in the Holy Spirit*, Jerry Jensen, editor. Logos International, 1976. Pp. 16-18, 31.

740 Greeley, Mary Ellen. "Charismatic Involvement for Religious," *Review for Religious*, 33 (May 1974): 601-608.

741 _____. "A Study of the Catholic Charismatic Renewal." Unpublished doctor's dissertation, University of St. Louis, 1973.

742 Green, E. "Phonological and Grammatical Aspects of Jargon in an Aphasic Patient: A Case Study," *Language and Speech*, 12 (1969): 103-13.

743 Green, Hollis Lynn. *Understanding Pentecostalism*. Pathway Press, 1970.

744 Green, Michael. *I Believe in the Holy Spirit*. Hodder & Stoughton, 1975.

745 Green, William M. "Glossolalia in the Second Century," *Restoration Quarterly*, 16 (1973): 231-39.

746 Greene, David. "The Gift of Tongues," *Bibliotheca Sacra*, 22 (January 1865): 99-126.

747 Grieve, A. J. "Charismata," in *Encyclopedia of Religion and Ethics*, James Hastings, editor. 12 vols. Scribner's Sons, 1955. 3: 368-72.

748 Griffiths, Michael C. *Three Men Filled with the Spirit: The Gift of Tongues*. Overseas Missionary Fellowship, 1969.

749 Grislis, Egil. "The Challenge of the Charismatic Renewal to Lutheran Thelogy," *Consensus*, 7 (October 1981): 3-25.

750 Gritsch, Eric W. *Born-Againism: Perspectives on a Movement*. Fortress Press, 1982.

751 Grom, B. "Die katholische charismatische Bewegung," *Stimmen der Zeit*, 191 (1973): 651-71.

752 Gromacki, Robert Glenn. *The Modern Tongues Movement*. Presbyterian and Reformed Publishing Company, 1967.

753 Gross, Don H. and Donald Hands. "A Charismatic Dictionary for Psychotherapists: Partial Translations of Popular Charismatic Phrases," *Journal for Pastoral Counseling*, 16 (Fall-Winter 1981): 32-34.

754 Grossmann, Siegfried. *Der Aufbruch: Charismatische Erneuerung in der katholischen Kirche*. Kassel, 1974.

755 _____. *Charisma, The Gifts of the Spirit*. Key Publishers, 1971.

756 Grossouw, W. "Glossolalie," *Bijbelsch Woordenboek*. Privately published,1941.

757 Grudem, Wayne. "1 Corinthians 14:20-25: Prophecy and Tongues as Signs of God's Attitude," *Westminster Theological Journal*, 41 (Spring 1979): 381-96.

758 _____. *The Gift of Prophecy in 1 Corinthians*. University Press of America, 1983.

759 Gründler, Johannes. *Lexikon der christlichen Kirchen und Sekten unter Berücksichtigung der Missionsgesellschaften und zwischenkirchlichen Organisationen*. Herder and Herder, 1961.

760 Grundmann, W. "Der Pfingstbericht der Apostelgeschichte in seinem theologischen Sinn," in *Studia Evangelica*, F. L. Cross, editor. Akademie-Verlag, 1964. Pp. 584-94.

761 Guder, Darrel L. "Die Jesus People begegnen die Kirche," *Evangelische Kommentare*, 5 (1972): 24-26.

762 Guillaume, Alfred. *Prophecy and Divination Among the Hebrews and Other Semites*. Hodder & Stoughton, 1938.

763 Guillet, J. *Viens, Esprit de Dieu*. Editions du Feu Nouveau, 1974.

764 Gulledge, Jack. "Jibberish Is Not a Gift!" *Western Recorder*, 145 (January 2, 1971): 11.

765 Gundry, Robert H. " 'Ecstatic Utterance' (N. E. B.)?" *Journal of Theological Studies*, 17 (October 1969): 299-307.

766 Gustafson, Robert R. *Authors of Confusion*. Grace Publishing Company, 1971.

767 Gutierrez, Lalei Elizabeth. "The Effects of Enhancement of Right Brain Functions Through Glossolalic Training on Nonverbal Sensitivity." Unpublished doctor's dissertation, Kent State University, 1980.

768 Gutman, Herbert G. "Protestantism and American Labor," *American Historical Review*, 72 (October 1966): 74-101.

H

769 Haanapfel, B. G. "A glossolalia no Novo Testamento," *Revista Ec-clesiastica Basileira*, 3 (1944): 51-66.

770 Haarbeck, Hermann. *Lass dir an meiner Gnade genügen. Die Stel-lungnahme des Gnadauer Verbandes zur Pfingstbewegung und zum Christlichen Germeinschaftsverband Mülheim.* Gnadauer Verlag, 1965.

771 Haavil, O. L. "Pentecostalism or the Tongues Movement," *Lutheran Herald*, (October 23 and 30, 1934): 935-37, 959-63.

772 Hagedorn, James W. "A Liberal Protestant Pastor Counsels with Conservative Catholic Charismatics," *Journal of Pastoral Care*, 35 (1981): 204-209.

773 Hagin, Kenneth E. *The Holy Spirit and His Gifts*. Privately pub-lished, n.d.

774 Haglof, Anthony. "Psychology and the Pentecostal Experience," *Spiritual Life*, 17 (Fall 1971): 198-210.

775 Haldeman, Isaac M. *Holy Ghost Baptism and Speaking with Tongues*. C. C. Cook, n.d.

776 Haley, Peter. "Rudolph Sohn on Charisma," *Journal of Religion*, 60 (April 1980): 185-97.

777 Hall, Mary. *A Quest for the Liberated Christian*. Peter Lang, 1978.

778 Hall, Robert B. *Receiving the Holy Spirit*. Privately published, n.d.

779 Hall, Thor. "A New Syntax for Religious Language," *Theology To-day*, 24 (July 1967): 172-84.

780 Halliday, Jerry. *Spaced Out and Gathered In*. Revell, 1972.

781 Halsema, J. H. van. "Mededeling: de historische betrouwbaarheid van het pinksterverhaal," *Nederlands Theologisch Tijdschrift*, 20 (February 1966): 218.

782 Hamilton, Michael P. *The Charismatic Movement*. Eerdmans, 1975.

783 Hamman, Adalbert. "La nouvelle Pentecôtes," *Bible et Vie chré-tienne*, 14 (1956): 82-90.

784 Handspicker, Meredith B. and Lukas Vischer, eds. *An Ecumenical Exercise* (Faith and Order 49). World Council of Churches, 1967.

785 Hanrahan, J. "Speaking in Tongues: Why in Our Day?" *Chelsea Journal*, (March-April 1978): 100.

786 Hanson, James H. "A Personal Experience," in "Symposium on Speaking in Tongues," *Dialog*, 2 (Spring 1963): 152-53.

787 Hardon, John A. "Pentecostalism: Evaluating a Phenomenon." Un-published paper, the Annual Conference for the Clergy, Arch-diocese of New York, April 1971.

788 Hargrave, Vessie D. "Glossolalia: Reformation to the Twentieth Century," in *The Glossolalia Phenomenon*, Wade H. Horton, ed-itor. Pathway Press, 1966. Pp. 97-139.

789 Hargrove, Barbara. "New Religious Movements and the End of the Age," *The Iliff Review*, 39 (Spring 1982): 41-52.

790 Harmon, George E. *The Gift of Tongues: What It Is and What It Is Not*. Faith Publishing House, n.d.

791 Harper, Charles L. "Old Testament Foundations of the Pentecostal Faith," *Pneuma*, 1:1 (Spring 1979): 21-30.

792 ————. "Society for Pentecostal Studies Presidential Address," *Pneuma*, 3:1 (Spring 1981): 48-53.

793 ————. "Spirit-Filled Catholics: Some Biographical Compari-sons," *Social Compass*, 21 (1974): 311-24.

794 Harper, Michael. *As At the Beginning: The Twentieth Century Pen-tecostal Revival*. Hodder & Stoughton, 1965.

795 ————. *The Baptism of Fire*. Logos International, n.d.

796 ————. *Bishop's Move: Six Anglican Bishops Share Their Ex-perience of Renewal*. Hodder & Stoughton, 1978.

797 ————. "Charismatic Renewal—A New Ecumenism?" *One in Christ*, 9:1 (1973): 59-65.

798 ————. *Life in the Holy Spirit: Some Questions and Answers*. Fountain Trust, 1966; Logos International, 1970.

799 ————. *Power for the Body of Christ*. Fountain Trust, 1964.

800 ————. *Prophecy, A Gift for the Body of Christ*. Logos Inter-national, 1970.

801 ————. *Walk in the Spirit*. Logos International, n.d.

802 Harpur, T. W. "Gift of Tongues and Interpretation," *Canadian Journal of Theology*, 12 (July 1966): 164-71.

803 Harrell, David E., Jr. *All Things Are Possible: The Healing and Charismatic Revivals in Modern America*. Indiana University Press, 1975.

804 Harrington, Daniel J. "Baptism in the Holy Spirit," *Chicago Studies*, 11:1 (1972): 31-44.

805 Harrington, Jeremy. *Jesus Superstar or Savior?* St. Anthony Messenger Press, 1972.

806 Harris, Carl. " 'Speaking in Tongues': A Point of Dissension," *The Dallas Morning Star*, 1 (June 28, 1964): 19.

807 Harris, Ralph W. *Spoken by the Spirit: Documented Accounts of "Other Tongues" from Arabic to Zulu*. Gospel Publishing House, 1973.

808 Harrison, Everett F. "The Holy Spirit in Acts and the Epistles," *Christianity Today*, 1 (May 27, 1957): 3-4.

809 Harrison, Irvine John. "A History of the Assemblies of God." Unpublished doctor's dissertation, Berkeley Baptist Divinity School, 1954.

810 Harrison, Michael I. "Maintenance of Enthusiasm: Involvement in a New Religious Movement," *Sociological Analysis*, 36 (Summer 1975): 150-60.

811 _____. "The Organization of Commitment in the Catholic Pentecostal Movement." Unpublished doctor's dissertation, University of Michigan, 1972.

812 _____. "Preparation for Life in the Spirit: The Process of Initial Commitment to a Religious Movement," *Urban Life and Culture*, 2 (1974): 387-414.

813 _____. "Sources of Recruitment to Catholic Pentecostalism," *Journal for the Scientific Study of Religion*, 13 (1974): 49-64.

814 Harrisville, Roy A. "Speaking in Tongues," *Sisters Today*, 50 (June-July 1974): 599-609.

815 _____. "Speaking in Tongues: A Lexicographical Study," *Catholic Biblical Quarterly*, 38 (January 1976): 35-48.

816 _____. "Speaking in Tongues—Proof of Transcendence?" *Dialog*, 13:1 (1974): 11-18.

817 Hart, Larry D. "Problems of Authority in Pentecostalism," *Review and Expositor*, 75 (Spring 1978): 249-66.

818 Häselbarth, Hans. *Charisma, Ordnungsprinzip der Kirche*. Herder annd Herder, n.d.

819 _____. "Die Zion Christian Church in evangelischer Sicht," in *Weltmission heute*, Peter Beyerhaus, editor. Edel, 1967. 33/34: 11-25.

820 Haskins, Dan D., Jr. "Glossolalia on Campus," *Collage*, 8 (1978): 4.

821 Hathaway, W. G. *Spiritual Gifts in the Church*. Elim Publishing Company, 1933.

822 Haufe, Christoph M. "Young Charismatics in Eastern Germany," *Lutheran World*, 22:4 (1975): 340-43.

823 Haughey, John C. "The Relationship Between Charismatic Authority and Church Office," *Theological Reflections on the Charismatic Renewal*, John C. Haughey, editor. Servant Books, 1978. Pp. 99-124.

824 Hauser, Markus. *Am Gnadenthrone: Gedanken über das Gebet nebst köstlichen Gebetserhörungen*. Private published, ca. 1897.

825 _____. *Kraft aus der Höhe. Zeugnisse für den Empfang des Heiligen Geistes*. 9th ed. Spener-Verlag, 1959.

826 _____. *Komme bald, Herr Jesus!* Privately published, 1903.

827 Hawkes, Paul D. *Pentecostalism in Canada: A History with Implications for the Future*. San Francisco Theological Seminary, 1983.

828 Hay, Alert L. "Flame in the Sanctuary," *The Pentecostal Herald*, (April 25, 1964): 14-15.

829 Hay, David and Ann Morisy. "Reports of Ecstatic, Paranormal, or Religious Experience in Great Britain and the United States," *Journal for the Scientific Study of Religion*, 17:3 (1978): 255-68.

830 Hayes, Doremus Almy. *The Gift of Tongues*. Jennings and Graham, 1913.

831 Haynes, Benjamin F. "Tongues," *Herald of Holiness*, 4 (June 23, 1915): 1-2.

832 Haywood, G. T. *Apostolic Bible Reading: The Birth of the Spirit and the Mystery of the Godhead*. Voice in the Wilderness Magazine, n.d.

833 Heath, Richard. "The Little Prophets of the Cevennes," *Contemporary Review*, 49 (January 1886): 117-31.

834 Hébert, Gérard. "Les sectes évangéligues et pentecôtistes," *Relations*, 20 (November 1960): 282-85.

835 Hefner, Philip. "Getting into the Spirit of Things," *Dialog*, 13:10 (1974): 25-32.

836 Hefren, H. C. *From Babel to Pentecost*. Faith Publishing House, n.d.

837 Hegy, Pierre. "Images of God and Man in a Catholic Charismatic Renewal Community," *Social Compass*, 25:1 (1978): 7-21.

838 Heiler, Friedrich. *Die Wahrheit Sundar Singhs: Neue Dokumente zum Sadhustreit*. Privately published, 1927.

839 Hein, Lorenz. "Philipp Jakob Spener, Ein Theologe des heiligen Geistes und Prophet der Kirche," in *Die Einheit de Kirche: Dimensionen ihrer Heiligkeit, Katholizität und Apostolizität*, H. Lorenz, editor. Steiner Verlag, 1977. Pp. 103-26.

840 Heitmann, Claus and Heribert Mühlen, eds. *Erfahrung und Theologie des Heiligen Geistes*. Kösel Verlag, 1974.

841 Hendricks, William L. "Glossolalia in the New Testament," in *Speaking in Tongues: Let's Talk about It*, Watson E. Mills, editor. Word Books, 1973. Pp. 48-60.

842 Hendrix, Scott. "Charismatic Renewal: Old Wine in New Skins," in *Currents in Theology and Missions*, 4 (June 1977): 158-66.

843 Hengel, Martin. *The Charismatic Leader and His Followers*. T. & T. Clark, 1981.

844 Henke, Frederick G. "Gift of Tongues and Related Phenomena at the Present Day," *American Journal of Theology*, 13 (April 1909): 193-206.

845 Henry, Carl F. H. *Contemporary Evangelical Thought: A Survey*. Baker Book House, 1968.

846 Hermanns, Jan Ranier. *Kennst du Jesus? Sozialreport über Jesus-Leute in Deutschland*. Kösel Verlag, 1972.

847 Hess, H. "A Study of Glossa in the New Testament," *Biblical Translator*, 15 (1964): 93-96.

848 Heuvel, Albert van den. "Challenge," *Ecumenical Courier*, 31:1 (1972): 4-5.

849 _____. "Die Jesus-Bewegung: Eine ökumenische Herausforderung," *Die Zeichen der Zeit*, 26 (1972): 189-90.

850 _____. "Jesus-People," *Risk*, 1 (1972): 16-20.

851 Heyer, Robert. *Pentecostal Catholics*. Paulist Press, 1974.

852 Hickman, James T. "Let's Find Pentecostal Balance," *Eternity* 25 (April 1974): 16-17.

853 Hiernaux, Jean P. and Jean Remy. "Socio-Political and Charismatic Symbolics: Cultural Change and Transactions of Meaning," *Social Compass*, 25:1 (1978): 145-63.

854 Higgins, Walter J. *Pioneering in Pentecost: My Experiences of 46 Years in the Ministry*. Privately published, 1958.

855 Hilgard, Ernest R. and Joseph R. Hilgard. *Hypnotic Susceptibility*. Harcourt, Brace and World, 1965.

856 Hilgenfeld, Adolf. *Die Glossolalie in der Alten Kirche*. Privately published, 1850.

857 Hill, David. "False Prophets and Charismatics: Structure and Interpretation in Matthew 7:15-23," *Biblica*, 57:3 (1976): 327-48.

858 Hill, Harold. *How Did It All Begin*. Logos International, 1976.

859 Hillis, Don W., ed. *Is the Whole Body a Tongue?* Eerdmans, 1974.

860 _____. *Tongues, Healing, and You*. Baker Book House, 1969.

861 _____. *What Can Tongues Do For You?* Moody Press, 1963.

862 Hillis, James W. "The New Pentecostalism," *Eternity*, 14 (July 1963): 17-18.

863 Hills, Aaron M. *The Tongues Movement*. Star Hall, n.d.

864 Hinders, J. T. and E. J. Martoch. "Pentecostalism," *Nuntius Aulae*, 4 (1961): 158-68.

865 Hinds, J. L. *The Modern Gift of Tongues Exposed*. Faith Publishing House, n.d.

866 Hine, Virginia. "Anthropological and Sociological Aspects of the Charismatic Renewal Movement within the Roman Catholic Church." Unpublished paper, Conference on Catholic Charismatic Renewal, Dayton, Ohio, June 1970.

867 _____. "Bridge-Burners: Commitment and Participation in a Religious Movement," *Sociological Analysis*, 31 (1970): 61-66.

868 _____. "The Deprivation and Disorganization Theories of Social Movements," in *Religious Movements in Contemporary America*, Irving I. Zaretsky and Mark P. Leone, editors. Princeton University Press, 1974.

869 _____. "Non-Pathological Pentecostal Glossolalia—A Summary of Psychological Literature." Unpublished report of the Pentecostal movement research committee, Department of Anthropology, University of Minnesota, 1967.

870 _____. "Pentecostal Glossolalia: Toward a Functional Interpretation," *Journal for the Scientific Study of Religion*, 8 (1969): 211-26.

871 _____. *Personal Transformation and Social Change: The Role of Commitment in a Modern Religious Movement*. Augsburg Publishing House, 1969.

872 Hine, Virginia H. and James H. Olila. "Interim Report on the Study of the Pentecostal Movement Conducted by the Anthropology Department of the University of Minnesota." Research report, University of Minnesota, 1967.

873 Hinson, E. Glenn. "A Brief History of Glossolalia," in *Glossolalia: Tongue Speaking in Biblical, Historical and Psychological Perspective*, Frank Stagg, E. Glenn Hinson, and Wayne E. Oates, editors. Abingdon Press, 1967. Pp. 45-75.

874 _____. "Morton T. Kelsey: Theologian of Experience," *Perspectives in Religious Studies*, 9 (Spring 1982): 5-20.

875 _____. "The Problem of Authority in Church and Society," *Review and Expositor*, 75 (Spring 1978): 177-293.

876 _____. "The Significance of Glossolalia in the History of Christianity," in *Speaking in Tongues: Let's Talk about It*, Watson E. Mills, editor. Word Books, 1973. Pp. 61-80.

877 Hitt, Russell T. "The New Pentecostalism: An Appraisal," *Eternity*, 14 (July 1963): 10-16.

878 Hitzer, Arnold. *Die Sogenannte "Apostolische Kirche," ihre Lehre und Ordnung*. Privately published, 1955.

879 Hobbs, Herschel H. *The Holy Spirit: Believer's Guide*. Broadman, 1967.

880 _____. "Tongues—Sign to Whom?" *Home Life*, 19 (1976): 1.

881 Hobsbaum, Eric J. *Primitive Rebels: Studies in Archaic Forms of Social Movements in the 19th and 20th Centuries*. N.p., 1959. 1959.

882 Hocken, Peter. "Catholic Pentecostalism: Some Key Questions," *The Heythrop Journal*, 15 (April-July 1974): 131-45.

883 _____. "Charismatic Renewal, the Churches and Unity," *One in Christ*, 15:4 (1979): 31-21.

884 _____. "Jesus Christ and the Gifts of the Spirit," *Pneuma*, 5:1 (Spring 1983): 1-16.

885 _____. "The Pentecostal-Charismatic Movement as Revival and Renewal," *Pneuma*, 3:1 (Spring 1981): 31-47.

886 ———. "Pentecostals on Paper," *The Clergy Review*, 59:11 (November 1974): 750-67; 60:3 (March 1975): 161-83; 60:6 (June 1975): 344-67.

887 ———. "Rapport à l'épiscopat anglais," *Vie Spirituelle*, 128 (January-February 1974): 31-42.

888 ———. "The Spirit and Charismatic Prayer," *Life and Worship*, 43 (1974): 1-10.

889 ———. "A Survey of the Worldwide Charismatic Movement," in *The Church is Charismatic: The World Council of Churches and the Charismatic Renewal*, Arnold Bittlinger, editor. World Council of Churches, 1981. Pp. 117-47.

890 Hodges, Melvin L. *Spiritual Gifts*. Gospel Publishing House, 1964.

891 Hodges, Serena M. *Look on the Fields: A Missionary Survey*. Gospel Publishing House, 1956.

892 Hodges, Zane C. "The Purpose of Tongues," *Bibliotheca Sacra*, 120 (July-September 1963): 226-33.

893 Hoekema, Anthony A. *Holy Spirit Baptism*. Eerdmans, 1972.

894 ———. "Holy Spirit in Christian Experience," *Reformed Review*, 28 (Spring 1975): 183-91.

895 ———. *Tongues and Spirit Baptism*. Baker Book House, 1970.

896 ———. *What About Tongue-Speaking?* Eerdmans, 1966.

897 Hoerber, Robert G. "New Wine in Old Bottles," *Concordia Theological Quarterly*, 41 (April 1977): 10-24.

898 Hollenweger, Walter J. "A Black Pentecostal Concept: A Forgotten Chapter of Black History," *Concept*, 30 (June 1970): Special Issue.

899 ———. *Charismatic and Pentecostal Movements: A Challenge to the Churches*. The Holy Spirit, 1974.

900 ———. "Charismatische und pfingstlerische Bewegung als Frage an die Kirchen heute," in *Wiederentdeckung des Heiligen Geistes*, M. Lienhard and H. Meyer, editors. Lembeck, 1974. Pp. 53-76.

901 ———. "Creator Spiritus: The Challenge of Pentecostal Experience to Pentecostal Theology," *Theology*, 81 (January 1978): 32-40.

902 ———. *Enthusiastisches Christentum: Die Pfingstbewegung in Geschichte und Gegenwart*. R. Brockhaus Verlag, 1966.

903 ———. *Erfahrungen der Leibhaftigkeit*. Kaiser, 1979.

904 _____. *The European Pentecostal Movement in Their Own Un-dersanding and the Understanding of Others*, World Council of Churches, n.d.

905 _____. "Evangelism and Brazilian Pentecostalism," *Ecumenical Review*, 20:2 (April 1968): 163-70.

906 _____. "Handbuch der Pfingstbewegung." 7 vols. Unpublished doctor's dissertation, University of Zurich, 1965.

907 _____. "Il risveglio Pentecostale in Italia: religione della fierezza dei poveri," *Concetto italiano*, 14 (May 1967): 19-32.

908 _____, ed. *Kirche, Benzin und Bohnensuppe. Auf den Spuren dynamischer Gemeinden*. TVZ, 1971.

909 _____. "Die kirch fuer andere: ein mythos," *Evangelische Theologie*, 37 (September-October 1977): 425-43.

910 _____. "Literatur von und uber die Pfingstbewegung (Weltkonferenzen, Holland, Belgien)," *Nederlands Theologisch Tijdschrift*, 18 (1963): 289-306.

911 _____. "A Little-Known Chapter in Pentecostal History," *Ecumenical Press Service*, (April 1970): 8f.

912 _____. "Methodism's Past in Pentecostalism's Present: A Case Study of a Cultural Clash in Chile," *Methodist History*, 20 (July 1982): 169-82.

913 _____. "O movimento pentecostal no Brasil," *Simpósio. Revista teológica da ASTE*, 2:3 (June 1963): 5-41.

914 _____. "El movimiento pentecostal y el movimiento ecuménico," *Estudios ecuméncios*, (April/May 1969): 11-14; *Concepto Latino-Americano*, 26 (March 1970): 12f.

915 _____. *New Wine in Old Wineskins: Protestant and Catholic Neo-Pentecostalism*. Fellowship Press, 1973.

916 _____. *Pentecost Between Black and White*. Christian Journals, Ltd., 1974.

917 _____. "Pentecost: When the Unthinkable Became Reality," *One World*, 67 (June 1981): 22.

918 _____. "The Pentecostal Movement and the WCC," *Ecumenical Review*, 18:3 (July 1966): 310-20.

919 _____. "Pentecostalism and Black Power," *Theology Today*, 30 (October 1973): 228-38.

920 _____. "Pentecostalism and the Third World," *Dialogue*, 9:2 (1970): 122-29.

921 _____. *The Pentecostals: The Charismatic Movement in the Churches*. Trans. R. A. Wilson. Augsburg Publishing House, 1972.

922 _____. *Die Pfingstkirchen: Selbstdarstellung Dokumente, Kommentare*. Evangelisches Verlagswerk, 1971.

923 _____. "Redécouvril le Pentecôtisme," *Communion*, 1:1 (1970): 74-78.

924 _____. "La researche de solidarite et d'authenticité dans les groupes de solidarité et les groupements souterrains," *Concilium*, 75 (1972): 65-75.

925 _____. "Roots and Fruits of the Charismatic Renewal in the Third World: Implications for Mission," *Theological Renewal*, 14 (February 1980).

926 _____. "Spiel als eine Form von Theologie. Zum geplanten Dialog mit der Pfingstbewegung," *Lutherische Monatschefte*, 9:10 (October 1970): 532-34.

927 _____. " 'Touching' and 'Thinking' the Spirit: Some Aspects of European Charismatics," in *Perspectives on the New Pentecostalism*, Russell F. Spittler, editor. Baker Book House, 1976. Pp. 44-50.

928 _____. "Unusual Methods of Evangelism in the Pentecostal Movement in China," *Monthly Letter on Evangelism*, (November-December 1965).

929 Holm, Lewis. "Speaking in Tongues," *The Lutheran Standard*, 2 (September 11, 1962): 3-6.

930 Holm, Nils G. "Functions of Glossolalia in the Pentecostal Movement," in *Psychological Studies on Religious Man*, Torvald Callstad, editor. Almkvist and Wiksell, 1978. Pp. 141-58.

931 _____. *Ritualistic Pattern and Sound Structure of Glossolalia in Material Collected in the Swedish-Speaking Parts of Finland*. Privately published, 1975.

932 _____. "Tungotal Och Andedop: En Religionspsykologisk undersökning av glossolali hos finlandssvenska pingstvänner." Unpublished doctor's dissertation, Uppsala Universitet, 1976.

933 Holmes, Urban T. *A History of Christian Spirituality: An Analytical Introduction*. The Seabury Press, 1980.

934 Holt, John B. "Holiness Religion: Cultural Shock and Social Reorganization," *American Sociological Review*, 5 (October 1940): 740-47.

935 "The Holy Ghost," *Time*, 76 (September 12, 1960): 71.

936 "Holy Spirit and Charismatic Theology: Papers Given at a Conference Held at Western Theological Seminary, November 1974," *Reformed Review*, 28 (Spring 1975): 147-227.

937 Hoover, Mario G. *Origin and Structural Development of the Assemblies of God*. Unpublished master's thesis, Southwest Missouri State College, 1968.

938 Hopkins, Evan, et al. *The Story of the Welsh Revival as Told by Eyewitnesses, Together with a Sketch of Evan Roberts and His Message to the World*. Revell, 1905.

939 Hopwood, P. G. S. *The Religious Experience of the Primitive Church*. Scribner's Sons, 1937.

940 Horn, William M. "Speaking in Tongues: A Retrospective Appraisal," *The Lutheran Quarterly*, 17 (November 1965): 316-29.

941 Horner, Kenneth A. "A Study of the Spiritual Gifts with Special Attention to the Gift of Tongues." Unpublished master's thesis, Faith Theological Seminary, 1945.

942 Horton, Harold. *The Gifts of the Spirit*. Redemption Tidings Bookroom, 1946.

943 _____. *The Gifts of the Spirit*. Assemblies of God Publishing House, 1954.

944 _____. *What is the Good of Speaking with Tongues?* Assemblies of God Publishing House, 1960.

945 Horton, Stanley M. *Tongues and Prophecy: How to Know a Gift of Utterance Is in Order*. Gospel Publishing House, 1972.

946 Horton, Wade H., ed. *The Glossolalia Phenomenon*. Pathway Press, 1966.

947 _____. *Pentecost: Yesterday and Today*. Pathway Press, 1964.

948 House, H. Wayne. "Tongues and the Mystery Religions of Corinth," *Bibliotheca Sacra*, 140 (April-June 1983): 134-50.

949 Howard, D. M. "Missionary Guidelines for Meeting a Charismatic Situation," *Evangelical Missions Quarterly*, 1 (Summer 1965): 18-25.

950 Howard, Richard E. *Tongues Speaking in the New Testament*. Western Maine Graphics Publications, 1980.

951 Howe, Claude L. "The Charismatic Movement in Southern Baptist Life," *Baptist History and Heritage*, 13 (June 1978): 20-27.

952 Howe, Leroy T. "Pentecostalism Today: Theological Reflections," *South East Asia Journal of Theology*, 18:1 (1977): 32-37.

953 Hoy, Albert L. "The Gift of Interpretation," *Paraclete*, 3 (Summer 1969): 28-31.

954 _____. *The Gift of Tongues*. Privately published, n.d.

955 _____. "Public and Private Uses of the Gift of Tongues," *Paraclete*, 2 (Fall 1968): 10-14.

956 Hoyt, Hermann. "Speaking in Tongues," *Brethren Missionary Herald*, 25 (1963): 156-57, 204-207.

957 Hubery, D. S. "Jesus Movement," *Expository Times*, 84 (April 1973): 212-14.

958 Huffman, Jasper A. *Speaking in Tongues*. Bethel Publishing Company, 1910.

959 Hughes, Philip Edgcumbe. "Review of Christian Religious Thought," *Christianity Today*, 6 (May 11, 1962): 63.

960 Hughes, Ray H. "Glossolalia in Contemporary Times," in *The Glossolalia Phenomenon*, Wade H. Horton, editor. Pathway Press, 1966. Pp. 143-77.

961 _____. "The New Pentecostalism: Perspective of a Classical Pentecostal Administrator," in *Perspectives on the New Pentecostalism*, Russell F. Spittler, editor. Baker Book House, 1976. Pp. 166-80.

962 _____. "A Traditional Pentecostal Looks at the New Pentecostals," *Christianity Today*, (June 7, 1974): 46.

963 Hull, C. L. "Handbuch der Pfingstbewegung."Unpublished doctor's dissertation, University of Zürich, 1965.

964 Hull, J. H. E. *The Holy Spirit in the Acts of the Apostles*. The World Publishing Company, 1968.

965 Hulme, A. J. Howard and Frederick H. Wood. *Ancient Egypt Speaks: A Miracle of Tongues*. Rider and Company, 1940.

966 Hummel, Charles E. *Fire in the Fireplace: Contemporary Charismatic Renewal*. Inter-Varsity Press, 1978.

967 Humphreys, Fisher and Malcolm Tolbert. *Speaking in Tongues*. Christian Litho, 1973.

968 Hunt, George L. *Speaking in Tongues*. Gospel Hall, n.d.

969 Hunter, Charles and Frances Hunter. *Why Should I Speak in Tongues?* Hunter Ministries Publishing Co., 1976.

970 Hunter, Harold. "Tongue-Speech: A Patristic Analysis," *Journal of Evangelical Theological Society*, 23:2 (1980): 125-37.

971 _____. *Spirit-Baptism: A Pentecostal Alternative*. University Press of America, 1983.

972 Hurst, D. V. "How to Receive the Baptism with the Holy Ghost," *The Pentecostal Evangel*, (April 26, 1964): 7-9.

973 Hurst, Wesley R., Jr. "Upon All Flesh," *The Pentecostal Evangel*, (May 2, 1965): 11-12.

974 Hutch, Richard A. "The Personal Ritual of Glossolalia," *Journal for Scientific Study of Religion*, 19:3 (1980): 255-66.

975 Hutchinson, Paul F. "Open Letter to Charismatic Lutherans," *Concordia Theological Monthly*, 43 (1972): 748-51.

976 Hutten, Kurth. *Seher, Grübler, Enthusiasten. Sekten und religiöse Sondergemeinschaften*. Quell-Verlag, 1950.

I

977 Inglis, James. "Gift of Tongues, Another View," *Theological Monthly*, 5 (1891): 425-27.

978 "Interesting Facts About the Assemblies of God," *The Pentecostal Evangel*, (September 16, 1962): 12.

979 International Church of the Foursquare Gospel. *Aimee Semple McPherson: Declaration of Faith*. Privately published, n.d.

980 _____. Annual Convention Report. Privately published, 1931.

981 _____. *The Four Square Gospel*. Raymond L. Cox for the Heritage Committee of the Foursquare Gospel Church, 1969.

982 _____. *History of Foursquaredom*. Privately published, n.d.

983 International Pentecostal Assemblies. *General Principles of the International Pentecostal Assemblies*. N.p., n.d.

984 _____. *Statement of Policy*. N.p., 1960.

985 Ironside, Henry A. *Apostolic Faith Missions and the So-Called Second Pentecost*. Loizeaux Brothers, n.d. (c. 1914-1916).

986 _____. *A History of the Brethren Movement*. Zondervan, 1942.

987 _____. *Holiness: The False and the True*. Loizeaux Brothers, 1964.

988 Irvine, William C., ed. *Heresies Exposed*. Privately published, 1940.

989 Irving, Edward. "On the Gifts of the Holy Ghost," in *The Collected Writings of Edward Irving*, G. Carlyle, editor. 5 vols. A. Strahan, 1864-1865. 5: 509-61.

990 Isbell, Charles D. "Glossolalia and Propheteilalia: A Study of 1 Corinthians 14," *Wesley Theological Journal*, 10 (Spring 1975): 15-22.

J

991 Jacob, Michael. *Pop Goes Jesus: An Investigation of Pop Religion in Britain and America*. Mowbrays, 1972.

992 Jacobs, Hayes B. "Oral Roberts: High Priest of Faith Healing," *Harper's*, 224 (February 1964): 37-43.

993 Jacquier, E. *Les Actes des Apôtres*. Paris, 1926. Cf. *Commentry*, pp. 54-57, 336-37, and *Excursus*, 7, pp. 187-95.

994 _____. "Zungenreden," *Die Religion in Geschichte und Gegenwart*. Privately published, 1931.

995 Jahr, Mary Ann. "First Pentecostal Abbey and the Ultimate Test," *Spirit*, (1976): 261-70.

996 Jaquith, James R. "Toward a Typology of Formal Communicative Behavior: Glossolalia," *Anthropological Linguistics*, 9 (1967): 1-8.

997 Jaschke, H. "Λαλεῖν bei Lukas," *Biblische Zeitschrift*, 15:8 (1971): 109-14.

998 Jauhiainan, Henry H. "Independent Pentecostal Church Movement," *Conviction*, 6 (March 1968): 6-7.

999 Jeffreys, George. "The Gospel of the Miraculous," in *The Phenomena of Pentecost*, Donald Gee, et al., editors. Gospel Publishing House, 1931. Pp. 33-50.

1000 _____. *The Miraculous Foursquare Gospel: Supernatural*. 2 vols. Elim Publishing Company, 1929/30.

1001 _____. *Why I Resigned from the Elim Movement*. Privately published, n.d.

1002 Jelly, Frederick M. "Mary and the Gifts and Charisms of the Spirit," in *Mary, the Spirit and the Church*, Vincent P. Branick, editor. Paulist Press, 1980. Pp. 79-91.

1003 Jennings, George. "An Ethnological Study of Glossolalia," *Journal of the American Scientific Affiliation*, 20 (March 1968): 5-16.

1004 Jensen, Jerry, ed. *Attorneys' Evidence on the Baptism in the Holy Spirit*. Full Gospel Business Men's Fellowship International, 1965.

1005 _____. *Baptists and the Baptism of the Holy Spirit*. Full Gospel Business Men's Fellowship International, 1963.

1006 _____, ed. *Catholics and the Baptism in the Holy Spirit*. Full Gospel Business Men's Fellowship International, 1968.

1007 _____, ed. *Charisma in the 20th Century Church*. Full Gospel Business Men's Fellowship International, 1968.

1008 _____, ed. *The Lutherans and the Baptism of the Holy Spirit*. Full Gospel Business Men's Fellowship International, 1963.

1009 _____. *Methodists and the Baptism of the Holy Spirit*. Full Gospel Business Men's Fellowship International, 1963.

1010 _____, ed. *Physicians, Examine the Baptism in the Holy Spirit*. Full Gospel Business Men's Fellowship International, 1967.

1011 _____. *Presbyterians and the Baptism of the Holy Spirit*. Full Gospel Business Men's Fellowship International, 1963.

1012 Jensen, Peter. "Calvin, Charismatics and Miracles," *The Evangelical Quarterly*, 51 (July-September 1979): 131-44.

1013 Jensen, Richard. *Touched by the Spirit: One Man's Struggle to Understand His Experience of the Holy Spirit*. Augsburg Publishing House, 1975.

1014 Jividen, Jimmy. *Glossolalia: From God or Man?* Star Publications, 1971.

1015 Johanson, Bruce C. "Tongues, A Sign for Unbelievers? A Structural and Exegetical Study of 1 Corinthians 14:20-25," *New Testament Studies*, 25 (January 1979): 180-203.

1016 Johansson, Nils. "1 Corinthians 14 and 1 Corinthians 15," *New Testament Studies*, 10 (April 1964): 383-92.

1017 Johnson, B. "Do Holiness Sects Socialize in Dominant Values?" *Social Forces*, 39 (1961): 309-16.

1018 Johnson, C. Lincoln and Andrew J. Weigert. "Emerging Faithstyle: A Research Note on the Catholic Charismatic Renewal," *Sociological Analysis*, 36 (Summer 1978): 165-72.

1019 Johnson, C. and J. Coalson. "Glossolalia and Internal-External Focus of Control," *Journal of Psychology and Theology*, (Fall 1977): 312.

1020 Johnson, Doyle P. "Dilemmas of Charismatic Leadership: The Case of the People's Temple," *Sociological Analysis*, 40 (Winter 1979): 315-23.

1021 Johnson, Merle Allison. *The Kingdom Seekers*. Abingdon Press, 1973.

1022 Johnson, Robert L. *Counter Culture and the Vision of God*. Augsburg Publishing House, 1971.

1023 Johnson, S. Lewis. "The Gift of Tongues and the Book of Acts," *Bibliotheca Sacra*, 120 (October-December, 1963): 309-11.

1024 Johnston, Benton. "Do Holiness Sects Socialize in Dominant Values?" *Social Forces*, 39 (1961-1962): 309-16.

1025 Jolley, Jennie A. *Bible Tongues*. Vantage Press, 1964.

1026 Jones, Charles Edwin. *A Guide to the Study of the Holiness Movement*. Scarecrow Press & American Theological Library Association, 1974.

1027 Jones, Eli S. *The Holy Spirit and the Gift of Tongues*. United Christian Ashrams, n.d.

1028 Jones, James W. "Charismatic Renewal After Kansas City," *Sojourners*, 6 (September 1977): 11-13.

1029 _____. *Filled with New Wine: The Charismatic Renewal of the Church*. Harper and Row, 1974.

1030 Jones, Kenneth E. *What about the Gift of Tongues?* Warner Press, 1962.

1031 Jones, Lawrence N. "The Black Pentecostal," in *The Charismatic Movement*, Michael Hamilton, editor. Eerdmans, 1975. Pp. 145-58.

1032 Jones, Pearl Williams. "A Minority Report: Black Pentecostal Women," *Spirit*, 1:2 (1977): 31-44.

1033 Jorstad, Erling T. *Bold in the Spirit: Lutheran Charismatic Renewal in America*. Augsburg Publishing House, 1974.

1034 _____. "The Grace that Amazes: From Drugs to Jesus," *Lutheran Forum*, 6:2 (1972): 16-20.

1035 _____, ed. *The Holy Spirit in Today's Church: A Handbook on the New Pentecostalism*. Abingdon Press, 1973.

1036 _____. "Pro and Con on the Charismatic Movement," *Christianity Today*, 23 (December 15, 1978): 34-35.

1037 _____. *That New-Time Religion*. Augsburg Publishing House, 1972.

1038 Joy, Donald M. *The Holy Spirit and You*. Light and Life Press, 1965.

1039 Joyce, J. Daniel. " 'Do All Speak With Tongues?'—No! 'Do Any Speak With Tongues?'—Maybe," *The Christian*, (May 30, 1971): 678-79.

1040 Judah, J. Stillson. *The History and Philosophy of Metaphysical Movements*. Westminster Press, 1967.

1041 Judisch, Douglas. *An Evaluation of Claims to the Charismatic Gifts*. Baker Book House, 1978.

1042 Juillerate, L. Howard. *Brief History of the Church of God*. Church of God Publishing House, 1922.

1043 Jung, Carl. *Psychology and Religion: West and East. The Collected Works of C. G. Jung*. Princeton University Press, 1969.

1044 Jungkuntz, Theodore. "Authority: A Charismatic Perspective," *Currents in Theology and Mission*, 3 (June 1976): 171-77.

1045 _____. "The Canon, the Charismata and the Cross," *The Cresset*, (1979): 25-29.

1046 _____. "Charismatic Worship: Challenge or Challenged?" *Response*, 16:1 (1976): 4-10.

1047 _____. *A Lutheran Charismatic Catechism*. Bread of Life Ministries, 1979.

1048 _____. "A Response to Scott Hendrix's 'Charismatic Renewal: Old Wine in New Skins,' " *Currents in Theology and Mission*, 5:1 (1978): 54-57.

1049 _____. "Secularization Theology, Charismatic Renewal, and Luther's Theology of the Cross," *Concordia Theological Monthly*, 42:1 (1971): 5-24.

K

1050 Kaasa, Harris. "An Historical Evaluation," in "Symposium on Speaking in Tongues," *Dialog*, 2 (1963): 156-58.

1051 Kampmeier, A. "Recent Parallels to the Miracle of Pentecost," *Open Court*, 22 (August 1908): 492-98.

1052 Kantzer, Kenneth S. "The Charismatics Among Us: The Christianity Today—Gallup Poll Identifies Who They Are and What They Believe," *Christianity Today*, 24 (February 22, 1980): 25-29.

1053 Karrenberg, F. and Klaus V. Bismarck, eds. *Verlorener Sonntag?* Kreuz-Verlag, 1959.

1054 Kasiera, E. Musembe. "Church's Service Ministry: A Pentecostal Response," *Missiology*, 4 (April 1976): 185-87.

1055 Kavanagh, Aidan. "Le ministère dans la communauté et dans la liturgie," *Concilium*, 72 (1972): 51-62.

1056 Kay, Thomas Oliver. "Pentecost: Its Significance in the Life of the Church." Unpublished master's thesis, Southern Baptist Theological Seminary, 1954.

1057 Keeling, Alma Lauder. "Not by Faith Alone: A Pentecostal Account of a Pentecostal Experience," *The Journal of Religion and Psychical Research*, 5 (January 1982): 50-53.

1058 Keilbach, W. "Zungenreden," in *Die Religion in Geschichte und Gegenwart*, Kurt Galling, editor. J. C. B. Mohr, 1962. 6: 1941-42.

1059 Keiper, R. L. "Tongues and the Holy Spirit," *Moody Monthly*, 64 (September 1963): 61-69.

1060 Kelsey, Morton T. "Courage, Unity and Theology," in *Perspectives on the New Pentecostalism*, Russell F. Spittler, editor. Baker Book House, 1976. Pp. 232-44.

1061 _____. *Discernment: A Study in Ecstasy and Evil*. Paulist Press, 1978.

1062 _____. *Dreams: The Dark Speech of the Spirit*. Doubleday and Company, 1968.

1063 _____. *Encounter with God*. Bethany, 1974.

1064 _____. *Healing and Christianity*. Harper and Row, 1973.

1065 _____. "Speaking in Tongues in 1971: An Assessment of Its Meaning and Value," *Review for Religious*, 30 (March 1971): 245-55.

1066 _____. *Tongue Speaking: An Experiment in Spiritual Experience*. Doubleday and Company, 1968. Pp. 246-52.

1067 Kendall, E. Lorna. "Speaking with Tongues," *Church Quarterly Review*, 168 (January-March 1967): 11-19.

1068 Kendrick, Klaude. "The Pentecostal Movement: Hopes and Hazards," *Christian Century*, 80 (1963): 608-10.

1069 _____. *The Promise Fulfilled: A History of the Modern Pentecostal Movement*. Gospel Publishing House, 1961.

1070 "The Key to Spiritual Discovery," *The Pentecostal Evangel*, (April 26, 1964): 2-3.

1071 Keyes, Frances P. *Tongues of Fire*. Coward-McCann, 1966.

1072 Kiev, Ari. "Psychotherapeutic Aspects of Pentecostal Sects Among West Indian Immigrants In England," *British Journal of Sociology*, 15 (1964): 129-38.

1073 _____. "The Study of Folk Psychiatry," in *Magic, Faith, and Healing: Studies in Primitive Psychiatry*, Ari Kiev, editor. Free Press, 1964.

1074 _____. *Magic, Faith and Healing*. Glencoe Press, 1964.

1075 Kildahl, John P. "Psychological Observations," in *The Charismatic Movement*, Michael Hamilton, editor. Harper and Row, 1975. Pp. 124-42.

1076 _____. *The Psychology of Speaking in Tongues*. Harper and Row, 1972.

1077 Kildahl, John P. and Paul Qualben. "Final Progress Report: Glossolalia and Mental Health." Unpublished paper. Brooklyn, n.d.

1078 _____. "Relationships Between Glossolalia and Mental Health." A report of a study done on a grant from the Behavioral Sciences Research Branch of the National Institute of Mental Health, 1971.

1079 Killian, Matthew. "Speaking in Tongues," *The Priest*, 25 (November 1969): 611-16.

1080 Kinder, Ernst. "Zur Lehre com Heiligen Geist nach den Lutherischen Bekenntnisschriften," *Fuldaer*, Hefte 15 (1964): 7-38.

1081 King, Joseph H. *From Passover to Pentecost*. Pentecostal Publishing House, 1914.

1082 _____. "History of the Fire Baptized Holiness Church," *Pentecostal Holiness Advocate*, (March 21-April 21, 1921): 5.

1083 King, Joseph H. and Blanche L. King. *Yet Speaketh, Memoirs of the Late Bishop Joseph H. King*. Pentecostal Publishing House, 1949.

1084 Kirkpatrick, Sherman. " 'Glossolalia' or 'the Gift of Tongues.' " Unpublished master's thesis, Phillips University, 1936.

1085 Klassen, D. "The Charismatic Confusion," *The Mennonite*, (October 23, 1973): 613.

1086 Klauser, Theodor. *Kleine abendländische Liturgiegeschichte. Bericht und Besingnung*. Mit zwei Anhängen: Richtlinien für die Gestaltung des Gotteshauses. Ausgewählte bibliographische Hinweise. Peter Hanstein, 1965.

1087 _____. *A Short History of the Western Liturgy*. Oxford University Press, 1969.

1088 Klein, W. C. *De loquendi formula "glōssais laleina."* Jena, 1816.

1089 _____. "The Church and Its Prophets," *Anglican Theological Review*, 44 (January 1962): 1-17.

1090 Klempnauer, Günther. *Christentum ist Brandstiftung. Jesus People im Kreuzfeuer*. R. Brockhaus-Verlag, 1972.

1091 Knight, Walter L. *Jesus People Came Alive*. Coverdale House, 1972.

1092 Knox, Lloyd H. *Key Biblical Perspectives on Tongues*. Light and Life Press, 1974.

1093 Knox, Ronald A. *Enthusiasm: A Chapter in the History of Religion with Special Reference to the 17th and 18th Centuries*. Oxford University Press, 1961.

1094 Knudsen, Ralph E. "Speaking in Tongues," *Foundations*, 9 (January-March 1966): 43-57.

1095 Koch, Kurt E. *Charismatic Gifts.* Association for Christian Evangelism, 1975.

1096 _____. *The Strife of Tongues.* Kregel Publications, 1969.

1097 Koenig, John. *Charismata: God's Gifts for God's People.* Westminster Press, 1978.

1098 _____. "Documenting the Charismatics," *Word World*, 1 (Summer 1981): 287-89.

1099 _____. "From Mystery to Ministry: Paul as Interpreter of Charismatic Gifts," *Union Seminary Quarterly Review*, 33:3/4 (1978): 167-74.

1100 _____. "Minneapolis: 1974 Conference on the Holy Spirit," *Lutheran World*, 21:4 (1974): 396-99.

1101 Koenker, E. Mark. "Lutheran/Charismatic Tensions in the Light of an Implicit Theology of the Cross in Acts," *Consensus: A Canadian Lutheran Journal of Theology*, 5 (January 1979): 26-32.

1102 Kooistra, Remkes. "I Would That Ye All Spake With Tongues," *Torch and Trumpet*, 14 (October 1964): 8-10.

1103 Kosick, F. J. *Pentecostal Power and Evidence.* N.p., n.d.

1104 _____. *Why Baptize in the Name of Jesus?* N.p., n.d.

1105 Kramer, Gustav. "Renewal of Prayer and Spirituality in Religious Communities and Movements," *Saint Mark's Reviw*, 73:5 (1973): 12-16.

1106 Krodel, Gerhard. "An Exegetical Examination," in "Symposium on Speaking in Tongues," *Dialog*, 2 (1963): 154-56.

1107 Kroll, Wilfried. *Commandos Jesus: La "Révolution de Jésus."* Editions Paulines, 1972.

1108 Kroll-Smith, Stephen J. "The Testimony as Performance: The Relationship of an Expressive Event to the Belief of a Holiness Sect," *Journal for the Scientific Study of Religion*, 19 (March 1980): 16-25.

1109 Kucharsky, D. E. "Testing Tongues: Luthern Medical Center Research Project," *Christianity Today*, 15 (June 4, 1971): 34-35.

1110 Kühn, Bernhard, ed. *Die Pfingstbewegung im Lichte der Heiligen Schrift und ihrer eigenen Geschichte.* Missionsbuchhandlung P. Ott, n.d.

1111 _____. "Zur Unterscheidung der Geister," in *Die sog. Pfingstbewegung*, H. Dallmeyer, editor. N.p., 1922. Pp. 23-40.

1112 Kulbeck, Gloria. *What God Has Wrought: A History of the Pente-costal Assemblies of Canada.* Pentecostal Assemblies of Canada, 1958.

1113 Kuyper, Abraham. *The Work of the Holy Spirit.* Trans. Henri De Vries. Eerdmans, 1956.

1114 Kydd, Ronald. "The Contribution of Denominationally Trained Clergymen to the Emerging Pentecostal Movement in Canada," *Pneuma*, 5:1 (Spring 1983): 17-33.

1115 _____. "Novatian's de Trinitate, 29: Evidence of the Charis-matic," *Scottish Journal of Theology*, 30:4 (1977): 313-18.

L

1116 Laan, Cornelis van der. "The Pentecostal Movement in Holland: Its Origin and Its International Position," *Pneuma*, 5:2 (Fall 1983): 30-38.

1117 LaBarre, Weston. *The Ghost Dance: The Origins of Religion*. Dell, 1972.

1118 _____. "Materials for a History of Studies of Crisis Cults: A Bibliographical Essay," *Current Anthropology*, 12 (1971): 3-44.

1119 _____. *They Shall Take Up Serpents: Psychology of Southern Snake Handling Cult*. University of Minnesota Press, 1962.

1120 LaBerge, Agnes N. Ozman. "History of the Pentecostal Movement from January 1, 1901." Unpublished typescript, n.d.

1121 _____. *What God Hath Wrought*. Herald Publishing Company, 1921.

1122 Lachat, W., ed. *Le Baptême dans l'Eglise réformée*. Textes commentés par un groupe de pasteurs. Privately published, 1954.

1123 Laffal, J. "Communication of Meaning in Glossolalia," *Journal of Social Psychology*, 92 (April 1974): 277-91.

1124 _____. "Language, Consciousness, and Experience," *The Psychoanalytic Quarterly*, 36 (1967): 61-66.

1125 _____. *Pathological and Normal Language*. Atherto Press, 1965.

1126 Lake, John G. *Die sichere Grundlage für die Heilung der Kranken und Gebrechlichen*. E. Weber, 1959.

1127 Lalive d'Epinay, Christian. *Le Pentecôtisme dans la société chilienne*. Essai d'approche sociologique, Geneva, 1967.

1128 Lambert, J. C. "Spiritual Gifts," in *The International Standard Bible Encyclopedia*. 5 vols. The Howard-Severance Company, 1915. 5: 2843-44.

1129 Lane, Ralph, Jr. "Catholic Charismatic Renewal," in *The New Religious Consciousness*, Charles Y. Glock and Robert N. Bellah, editors. University of California Press, 1976. Pp. 162-79.

1130 _____. "Catholic Charismatic Renewal Movement in the United States: A Reconsideration," *Social Compass*, 25:1 (1978): 23-35.

1131 Lang, G. H. *The Earlier Years of the Modern Tongues Movement.* Privately published, n.d.

1132 _____. *The Modern Gift of Tongues: Whence Is It? A Testimony and an Examination.* Marshall Brothers, 1913.

1133 Lange, Joseph. "Relationship of the Charismatic Renewal to the Institutional Church," *Moravian Theological Seminary Bulletin*, (1972-1977): 13-19.

1134 Lankford, John. "David Edwin Harrell, Jr., All Things Are Possible: The Healing and Charismatic Revivals in Modern America: A Review Essay," *Historical Magazine of the Protestant Episcopal Church*, 46 (June 1977): 251-65.

1135 Laporte, Jean. "The Holy Spirit, Source of Life and Activity in the Early Church," in *Perspectives on Charismatic Renewal*, Edward D. O'Connor, editor. University of Notre Dame Press, 1975. Pp. 57-99.

1136 Lapsley, James N. and John H. Simpson. "Speaking in Tongues," *Princeton Seminary Bulletin*, 58 (February 1965): 1-18.

1137 _____. "Speaking in Tongues: Infantile Babble or Song of the Self?" *Pastoral Psychology*, 15 (September 1964): 16-24.

1138 _____. "Speaking in Tongues: Token of Group Acceptance and Divine Approval," *Pastoral Psychology*, 15 (May 1964): 48-55.

1139 Laski, Margharita. *Ecstasy: A Study of Some Secular and Religious Experiences.* Indiana University Press, 1961.

1140 Latte, Kurt. "The Coming of the Pythia," *The Harvard Theological Review*, 33 (1940): 9-18.

1141 Laughlin, Henry P. *The Neurosis in Clinical Practice.* W. B. Saunders, 1956.

1142 Laurentin, René. "The Charismatic Movement: Prophetic Renewal or Neo-Conservatism?" *Neo-Conservatism: Social and Religious Phenomenon*, Gregory Baum, editor. The Seabury Press, 1981. Pp. 25-32.

1143 _____. "Charismatische Erneuerung: Prophetische Erneuerung oder Neokonservatismus?" *Concilium*, 17:1 (1981): 27-33.

1144 _____. "Mary: Model of the Charismatic as Seen in Acts 1-2, Luke 1-2, and John," in *Mary, the Spirit and the Church*, Vincent P. Branick, editor. Paulist Press, 1980. Pp. 28-43.

1145 _____. *Pentecôtisme chez les catholiques*. Beauchesne, 1974.

1146 Lawrence, Bennet F. *The Apostolic Faith Restored*. Gospel Publishing House, 1916.

1147 LeBaron, Albert. "A Case of Psychic Automatism, Including 'Speaking with Tongues,' " *Proceedings of the Society for Psychical Research*, 12 (1896-1897): 277.

1148 Le Barre, Weston. "Speaking in Tongues: Token of Group Acceptance and Divine Approval," *Pastoral Psychology*, 15 (May 1964): 48-55.

1149 _____. *They Shall Take Up Serpents: Psychology of the Southern Snake-Handling Cult*. University of Minnesota Press, 1962.

1150 Lebeau, P. "Le renouveau charismatique dans l'Église." Conference to the second meeting of the leaders of charismatic groups, at Magnificat House in Kovenjoel, Belgium, March 2, 1974.

1151 Leberle, H. I. "Be Filled With the Spirit of Love: An Update on the State of the Charismatic Renewal and Some Reflections on its Central Experiential Teachings," *Evangelische Theologie*, 15:3 (December 1982): 33-48.

1152 Lebra, Takie S. "Milleranian Movements and Resocialization," *American Behavioral Scientist*, 16 (1972): 195-217.

1153 Le Braz, B. M. "Regards sur le Renouveau charismatique," *Cahiers marials*, 90 (November 15, 1973): 355-71.

1154 Lechler, Alfred. *Die Pfingsthewegung in Deutschland in ärztlich-seelsorgerlicher Sicht*. N.p., 1962.

1155 _____. *Zum Kampf gegen die Pfingstbewegung*. 2nd ed. Bundes-Verlag, n.d.

1156 Leclercq, H. "Glossolalie," *Dictionnarie d'archéologie chrétienne et de liturgie*, 6 (1924): 1322-27.

1157 Lederly, H. I. "Be Filled with the Spirit of Love: An Update on the State of the Charismatic Renewal and Some Reflections on Its Central Experiental Teaching," *Theologia Evangelica*, 15:3 (December 1982): 33-48.

1158 Leech, Kenneth. "The Hippies and Beyond," *The Churchman*, 16 (1972): 82-92.

1159 Lehmann, Jürgen. *Die Kleinen Religionsgemeinchaften des öffentlichen Rechtes im heutigen Staatskirchenrecht*. N.p., 1959.

1160 Lemonnyer, A. "Charismes," *Dictionnaire de la Bible: Supplément*, 1 (1928): 1233-43.

1161 Lemons, Frank W. *Our Pentecostal Heritage*. Pathway Press, 1963.

1162 Lensch, Rodney. *My Personal Pentecost*. Impact Books, 1972.

1163 Lenski, Gerhard. "Social Correlates of Religious Interest," *American Sociological Review*, 18 (1953): 533-44.

1164 Lepargneur, Francisco. "Reflexões católicas em face do Movimento Pentecostal no Brasil," *O Espírito Santo*, ASTE (1966): 47-67.

1165 Lepesant, B. and L. Fabre. "Les oasis de l'Esprit," *Parole et Mission: Dossier 6*, (1973): 81-84.

1166 Lesêtre, H. "Langues (Don des)," *Dictionnaire de la Bible*, 4 (1908): 74-81.

1167 *Les Mouvements de Pentecôte*. Trans. Frank van het Hof. Delachaux et Niestlé, 1964.

1168 Lesser, R. H. *The Holy Spirit and the Charismatic Renewal*. Theological Publications in India, 1978.

1169 Lester, Andrew D. "Glossolalia: A Psychological Evaluation." Unpublished seminar paper, Southern Baptist Theological Seminary, 1965.

1170 Letis, Theodore P. *Martin Luther and Charismatic Ecumenism*. Reformation Research Press, 1979

1171 Lewis, I. M. *Ecstatic Religion: An Anthropological Study of Spirit Possession and Shamanism*. Pelikan Books, 1971.

1172 Lhermitte, Jacques Jean. *True and False Possession*. Trans. P. J. Hepburne-Scott. Hawthorne Books, 1963.

1173 Lightner, Robert Paul. *Speaking in Tongues and Divine Healing*. Regular Baptist Press, 1965.

1174 _____. *The Tongues Tide*. Empire State Baptist Fellowship, 1964.

1175 Liias, Jurgen W. "Charismatic Power or Military Power," *The Christian Century*, 100 (November 30, 1983): 1110-13.

1176 Lillie, David George. *Tongues Under Fire*. Fountain Trust, 1966.

1177 Limbeck, M. "Pfingsten: Der Hl. Geist und die Kirche," *Lebendige Seelsorge*, 10 (1969): 232-45.

1178 Lindberg, Carter. *The Third Reformation? Charismatic Movements and the Lutheran Tradition*. Mercer University Press, 1983.

1179 Lindberg, D. Robert. "Try the Spirits," *Presbyterian Guardian*, 34 (February 1965): 19-24.

1180 Linder, Robert D. "Ireland's Charismatics: Planting Seeds of Unity," *Christianity Today*, 19 (September 26, 1975): 45-47.

1181 Lindsay, George. *Twenty-One Reasons Why Christians Should Speak in Other Tongues*. Voice of Healing Publishing Company, 1959.

1182 Lindsay, Gordon. *All About the Gifts of the Spirit*. N.p., n.d.

1183 _____. *The Gift of Prophecy and the Gift of Interpretation of Tongues*. Voice of Healing Publishing Company, 1964.

1184 Lindsell, Harold. "Tests for the Tongue Movement," *Christianity Today*, (December 8, 1972): 8.

1185 _____. "Tests for the Tongues Movement," in *Is the Whole Body a Tongue?* Don W. Hillis, editor. Eerdmans, 1974.

1186 Litell, Franklin H. "Free Churches and the Pentecostal Challenge," *Journal of Ecumenical Studies*, 5 (Winter 1968): 131-32.

1187 Lockyer, Herbert. "The Day of Pentecost," *Evangelical Christian*, 54 (May 1958): 209-10.

1188 Loewenich, Walter von. "Das christliche Menschenbild im Umbruch der Moderne," in *Der Pietismus in Gestalten und Wirkungen*. Luther Verlag, 1975. Pp. 326-42.

1189 _____. "Luthers Auslegung des Pfingstgeschichte," in *Vierhundertfünfzip Jahre lutherische Reformation 1517-1967. Fetschrift für Franz Lau*. Vandenhoeck & Ruprecht, 1967. Pp. 181-90.

1190 Logan, James C. "Controversial Aspects of the Movement," in *The Charismatic Movement*, Michael Hamilton, editor. Eerdmans, 1975. Pp. 33-46.

1191 *Logos: An International Charismatic Journal*. Logos International.

1192 Lohmann, E. *Pfingstbewegung und Spiritismus*. Verlag Orient-Buchhandlung des Deutschen Hülfsbundes für christliches Liebeswerk im Orient, 1910.

1193 Lohse, Eduard. "Pentecost," in *Theological Dictionary of the New Testament*, Gerhard Kittell, editor. Trans. Geoffrey W. Bromiley. 9 vols. Eerdmans, 1964-1976. 6: 44-53.

1194 Lombard, Émile. "Essai d'une classification des phénomènes de glossolalie," *Archives de Psychologie*, 7 (1908): 1-62.

1195 _____. *De la Glossolalie chez les premiers chrètiens et des phénomènes similaires*. Bridel, 1910.

1196 _____. "La glossolalie à notre époque," *Journal de Genève*, (December 3, 1911).

1197 _____. "Le parler en langues à Corinthe d'apreès les textes de saint Paul et les analogies modernes," *Revue de théologie et de philosophie*, 42 (1909): 5-52.

1198 Longenecker, Bill. "An Evaluation of the Jesus Movement in Lancaster County Pennsylvania," *Brethren Life and Thought*, 17:3 (1972): 179-80.

1199 Lotze, Wilhelm. "Dowie und die christlich-katholische Kirche in Zion," in *Kirchen und Sekten der Gegenwart*, Ernst Kalb, editor. Gesellschaft, 1905. Pp. 485-92.

1200 Loud, Grover C. *Evangelized America*. Dial, 1928.

1201 Lovekin, Arthur Adams. "Glossolalia: A Critical Study of Alleged Origins, the New Testament and the Early Church." Unpublished master's thesis, University of the South, 1962.

1202 Lovekin, Adams and Newton Malony. "Religious Glossolalia: A Longitudinal Study of Personality Changes," *Journal for the Scientific Study of Religion*, 16 (December 1977): 383-93.

1203 Lovett, Leonard. "Black Origins of the Pentecostal Movement," in *Aspects of Pentecostal-Charismatic Origins*, Vinson Synan, editor. Logos International, 1975. Pp. 123-41.

1204 _____. "Perspective on the Black Origins of the Contemporary Pentecostal Movement," *Journal of the Interdenominational Theological Center*, 1 (Fall 1973): 36-49.

1205 Lowe, Harry W. *Speaking in Tongues: A Brief History of the Phenomenon Known as Glossolalia, or Speaking in Tongues*. Pacific Press Publishing Association, 1965.

1206 Lowry, Oscar. *The Pentecostal Baptism and the Enduement of Power*. Moody Press, 1936.

1207 Ludwig, Arnold M. "The Trance," *Comprehensive Psychiatry*, 8 (1967): 7-15.

1208 "Lutherans, The Spirit, The Gifts, and The World." Privately published, 1973.

1209 Lynd, Robert S. and Helen Merrell Lynd. *Middletown*. Harcourt, Brace & World, 1956.

1210 Lyon, Robert W. "Baptism and Spirit Baptism in the New Testament," *Wesley Theological Journal*, 14 (Spring 1979): 14-26.

1211 Lyonnet, S. "De glossolalia Pentecotes eiusque Significatione," *Verbum domini*, 24 (1944): 65-75.

1212 Lyra, Jorge Buarque. *O movimento pentecostal no Brasil. Profilaxia cristã dêsse movimento em defesa de "O Brasil Para Cristo."* Privately published, 1964.

1213 _____. *Orientaçâo Evngélica (Interdenominacional) para salvar o Brasil*. Privately published, 1960.

1214 Lyra, S. "Rise and Development of the Jesus Movement," *Calvin Theological Journal*, 8 (April 1973): 40-61.

M

1215 MacArthur, John F., Jr. "The Charismatics," *Moody Monthly*, 80 (December 1979): 82-85.

1216 _____. *The Charismatics*. Zondervan, 1978.

1217 McCandlish, Phillips. "And There Appeared Unto Them Tongues of Fire," *Saturday Evening Post*, (May 16, 1964): 30.

1218 McCasland, S. V. "Signs and Wonders," *Journal of Biblical Literature*, 76 (June 1957): 149-52.

1219 _____. "Spirit," in *The Interpreter's Dictionary of the Bible*, George Arthur Buttrick, editor. 4 vols. Abingdon Press, 1962. R-Z: 432-34.

1220 McCone, R. Clyde. *Culture and Controversy: An Investigation of the Tongues of Pentecost*. Dorrance, 1978.

1221 _____. "The Phenomena of Pentecost," *Journal of the American Scientific Affiliation*, 23 (September 1971): 83-88.

1222 McCready, William. "Les nouveaux pentecôtistes," *Concilium*, 72 (1972): 107-11.

1223 McCrossan, Thomas J. *Are All Christians Baptized with the Holy Ghost at Conversion?* Privately published, 1932.

1224 _____. *Speaking with Other Tongues: Sign or Gift—Which?* Christian Alliance Publishing Company, 1919.

1225 MacDonald, John. *Jesus in Haight Ashbury*. Aussaat, 1972.

1226 MacDonald, William G. "Exegetical Circles: Innovation at Charlotte Meeting of Society for John's Pentecostal Studies: Report on 'Spirit and Regeneration in John's Gospel,' " *Pneuma*, 4:1 (Spring 1982): 19-31.

1227 _____. "Glossolalia in the New Testament," *Bulletin of the Evangelical Theological Society*, 7 (Spring 1964): 59-68.

1228 _____. "Pentecostal Theology: A Classical Viewpoint," in *Perspectives on the New Pentecostalism*, Russell F. Spittler, editor. Baker Book House, 1973. Pp. 58-74.

1229 _____. "The Place of Glossolalia In Neo-Pentecostalism," in *Speaking in Tongues: Let's Talk about It*, Watson E. Mills, editor. Word Books, 1973. Pp. 81-93.

1230 McDonnell, Kilian. *Baptism in the Spirit as an Ecumenical Problem*. Notre Dame, 1972.

1231 _____. "Catholic Charismatic Renewal: Reassessment and Critique," *Religion in Life*, 44 (Summer 1975): 138-54.

1232 _____. "Catholic Charismatics," *Commonweal*, 96 (May 5, 1972): 207-11.

1233 _____. "Catholic Pentecostalism: Problems in Evaluating," *Dialog*, 9 (Winter 1970): 35-54.

1234 _____. *Charismatic Renewal and the Churches*. The Seabury Press, 1976.

1235 _____. *The Charismatic Renewal and Ecumenism*. Paulist Press, 1978.

1236 _____. "Die charismatische Bewegung in der Katholischen Kirche," in *Weigerentgeckung des Reiligen Ristes*, R. Meyer, editor. Lembeck, 1974.

1237 _____. "Classical Pentecostalism/Roman Catholic Dialogue: Hopes and Possibilities," in *Perspectives on the New Pentecostalism*, Russell F. Spittler, editor. Baker Book House, 1976. Pp. 246-68.

1238 _____. "The Distinguishing Charcteristics of the Charismatic-Pentecostal Spirituality," *One in Christ*, 10:2 (1974): 117-28.

1239 _____. "The Ecumenical Significance of the Pentecostal Movement," *Worship*, 40 (1966): 608-29.

1240 _____. "Eucharistic Celebrations in the Catholic Charismatic Movement," *Studie Liturgica*, 9 (1973): 19-44.

1241 _____. "The Experience of the Holy Spirit in the Catholic Charismatic Renewal," *Conflicts about the Holy Spirit*. The Seabury Press, 1979. Pp. 95-102.

1242 _____. "The Experiential Roman Catholic-Pentecostal Dialogue," *One in Christ*, 9:1 (1973): 43-58.

1243 _____. "The Experiential and the Social: New Models from the Pentecostal/Roman Catholic Dialogue," *One in Christ*, 9:1 (1973): 43-58.

1244 ——————. "Holy Spirit and Pentecostals," *Commonweal*, 89 (November 8, 1968): 198-204.

1245 ——————. "The International Roman Catholic-Pentecostal Dialogue," *One in Christ*, 10:1 (1974): 4-6.

1246 ——————. "New Dimensions in Research on Pentecostalism," *Worship*, 45 (April 1971): 214-19.

1247 ——————. "Pentecostal Culture: Protestant and Catholic," *One in Christ*, 7:4 (1971): 310-18.

1248 ——————. "Pentecostalism: A Selected Bibliography," *One in Christ*, 10:1 (1974): 96-99.

1249 ——————. *Presence, Power, Praise: Documents on the Charismatic Renewal*. 3 vols. Liturgical Press, 1980.

1250 ——————. "The Relationship of the Charismatic Renewal to the Established Denominations," *Dialogue*, 13:3 (1974): 223-29.

1251 ——————. "A Sociologist Looks at the Catholic Charismatic Renewal," *Worship*, 49 (August-September 1975): 378-92.

1252 ——————. "Statement of the Theological Basis of the Catholic Charismatic Renewal," *Worship*, 47 (December 1973): 610-20.

1253 ——————. *Statement of the Theological Principles of the Catholic Charismatic Movement*. Dove Publications, 1973.

1254 ——————. "Towards a Critique of the Churches and the Charismatic Renewal," *One in Christ*, 16:4 (1980): 329-37.

1255 McDonnell, Kilian and Arnold Bittlinger. *The Baptism in the Holy Spirit as an Ecumenical Problem*. Charismatic Renewal Services, 1972.

1256 McEwen, J. S. "The Ministry of Healing," *Scottish Journal of Theology*, 7 (1954): 133-52.

1257 McGaw, Douglas B. "Commitment and Religious Community: A Comparison of a Charismatic and a Mainline Congregation," *Journal for the Scientific Study of Religion*, 18 (June 1979): 146-63.

1258 ——————. "Meaning and Belonging in a Charismatic Congregation: An Investigation into Sources of Neo-Pentecostal Success," *Review of Religious Research*, 21 (Summer 1980): 284-301.

1259 McGee, John V. *Talking in Tongues*. W. Smith Publishers, 1963.

1260 MacGorman, J. W. "Glossolalic Error and Its Correction: 1 Corinthians 12-14," *Review and Expositor*, 80:3 (Summer 1983): 389-400.

1261 McGuire, Kenneth. "Affective Deprivation as a Factor in Crisis Movement Formation: A Current Example." Paper presented at the meeting of the Society for the Scientific Study of Religion, San Francisco, 1973.

1262 McGuire, Meredith B. "An Interpretive Comparison of Elements of the Pentecostal and Underground Church Movements in American Catholicism," *Sociological Analysis*, 35 (1974): 57-63.

1263 _____. *Pentecostal Catholics: Power, Charisma and Order in a Religious Movement.* Temple University Press, 1981.

1264 _____. "Sharing Life in the Spirit: The Function of Testimony in Catholic Pentecostal Commitment and Conversion." Paper presented at the meeting of the Society for the Scientific Study of Religion, Milwaukee, 1975.

1265 _____. "Social Context of Prophecy: 'Word-Gifts' of the Spirit Among Catholic Pentecostals," *Review of Religious Research*, 19 (Spring 1977): 73-85.

1266 _____. "Social Context of Prophecy: 'Word-Gifts' of the Spirit Among Catholic Pentecostals," *Review of Religious Research*, 18 (Winter 1977): 134-47.

1267 _____. "Speaking of the Spirit: Language Use by Catholic Pentecostals." Unpublished report to the World Congress of Sociology, Research Committee on Sociolinguistics, 1974.

1268 _____. "Testimony as a Commitment Mechanism in Catholic Pentecostal Prayer Groups," *Journal for the Scientific Study of Religion*, 16 (June 1977): 165-68.

1269 _____. "Toward a Sociological Interpretation of the Catholic Pentecostal Movement," *Review of Religious Research*, 16 (1975): 94-104.

1270 McKay, J. R. "A Critique of Pentecostalism," *Church Quarterly*, 3 (1971): 311-17.

1271 McKay, John W. "Elihu: A Proto-Charismatic?" *Expository Times*, 90 (March 1979): 167-71.

1272 Mackey, C. Lloyd. "Pentecostals Proliferate and Bridge Barriers," *Christianity Today*, 23 (November 2, 1979): 61-63.

1273 Mackie, Alexander. *The Gift of Tongues.* George H. Doran Company, 1921.

1274 McKinney, Joseph. "The Gift of Tongues: A School for Prayer and Ministry," *New Covenant*, 10:12 (June 1981): 12-15.

1275 McLoughlin, William G. "Is There a Third Force in Christendom?" *Daedalus*, 96 (Winter 1967): 43-68.

1276 McNamee, John J. "The Role of the Spirit in Pentecostalism: A Comparative Study." Unpublished doctor's dissertation, University of Tübingen, 1974.

1277 MacNutt, Francis. *Healing*. Ave Maria Press, 1974.

1278 _____. "Resting in the Spirit," *Catholic Charismatic*, 2:4 (1977): 18-23.

1279 McTernan, J. "Water Baptism: A Response to Fr. Kilian McDonnell's Paper," *One in Christ*, 10 (1974): 203-205.

1280 Maeder, Alphonse. "La Langue d'un Aliene: Analyse d'un Cas de Glossolalie," *Archives de Psychologie*, 9 (March 1910): 208-16.

1281 Maher, Brian. "Catholic Pentecostalism," *Reality*, 37 (1973): 14-171, 33-36.

1282 Malony, H. Newton. "Debunking Some of the Myths about Glossolalia," *Journal of the American Scientific Affiliation*, 34:3 (September 1982): 144-48.

1283 Malony, H. Newton, Nelson Zwaanstra and James W. Ramsey. "Personal and Situational Determinants of Glossolalia: A Literature Review and Report of Ongoing Research." Paper presented at the International Congress of Religious Studies, Los Angeles, 1972.

1284 Maly, K. "Apostolische Gemeindeführung," *Theologie der Gegenwart*, 10 (1967): 219-22.

1285 _____. *Mündige Gemeinde*. Privately published, 1967.

1286 Manaranche, André. "Dieu, Jésus, l'Esprit," *Cahiers de l'actualité religieuse et sociale*, 47 (1972): 711-18.

1287 Marrow, James Alston. "The Holy Spirit in the Book of Acts." Unpublished master's thesis, Union Theological Seminary, 1952.

1288 Marshall, I. Howard. "The Significance of Pentecost," *Asbury Seminarian*, 32 (April 1977): 17-39.

1289 Martin, Francis. "The Charismatic Renewal and Biblical Hermeneutics," in *Theological Reflections on the Charismatic Renewal*, John C. Haughey, editor. Servant Books, 1978. Pp. 1-37.

1290 Martin, Ira J. "1 Corinthians 13 Interpreted by Its Context," *The Journal of Bible and Religion*, 18 (April 1950): 101-105.

1291 _____. "Glossolalia," *Journal of Biblical Literature*, 63 (1944): 123-30.

1292 _____. "Glossolalia in the Apostolic Church," *Journal of Biblical Literature*, 63 (1944): 123-30.

1293 _____. *Glossolalia in the Apostolic Church: A Survey Study of Tongue Speech*. Berea College Press, 1960.

1294 _____. *Glossolalia, the Gift of Tongues: A Bibliography*. Pathway Press, 1970.

1295 _____. "The Place and Significance of Glossolalia in the New Testament." Unpublished doctor's dissertation, Boston University, 1942.

1296 Martin, Marie-Louise. "Afrikaischer Messianismus und der Messias der biblischen Offenbarung," *Weltmission heute*, 33:34 (1967): 40-56.

1297 _____. *The Biblical Concept of Messianism and Messianism in Southern Africa*. Unpublished doctor's dissertation, University of South Africa, 1964.

1298 _____. *Critical Notes on W. J. Hollenweger's Dissertation*. Lesotho, 1964.

1299 Martin, Ralph. "Baptism in the Holy Spirit: Pastoral Implications," in *The Holy Spirit and Power*, Kilian McDonnell, editor. Doubleday and Company, 1975. Pp. 91-105.

1300 _____. "A Catholic Assesses Charismatic Renewal in His Church," *Christianity Today*, 24 (March 7, 1980): 18-20.

1301 _____. *Spirit and the Church: Personal and Documentary Record of the Charismatic Renewal, and the Ways it is Bursting to Life in the Catholic Church*. Paulist Press, 1976.

1302 Marty, Martin. "Pentecostalism in the Context of American Piety and Practice," in *Aspects of Pentecostal-Charismatic Origins*, Vinson Synan, editor. Logos International, 1975. Pp. 193-233.

1303 Maskrey, Cyril H. *The Pentecostal Error*. Light Publishing Company, 1953.

1304 Massee, J. C. *The Holy Spirit*. Revell, 1940.

1305 Masserano, Frank C. "A Study of the Worship Forms of the Assemblies of God Denomination." Unpublished master's thesis, Princeton Theological Seminary, 1966.

1306 Matthews, John. *Speaking in Tongues*. Privately published, 1925.

1307 Matzat, Don. *Serving the Renewal: Stories of the Men of Lutheran Charismatic Renewal Services*. Bread of Life Ministries, 1978.

1308 Mauro, Philip. *Speaking in Tongues*. Reiner Publications, n.d.

1309 Maury, Philippe. *Politics and Evangelism*. Doubleday and Company, 1959.

1310 Maust, John. "Charismatic Leaders Seeking Faith for Their Own Healing (and) the Secret Summit Reconstructed (1975)," *Christianity Today*, 24 (April 4, 1980): 44-46.

1311 Mawn, Benedict Joseph. "Testing the Spirits: An Empirical Search for the Soico-Cultural Situational Roots of the Catholic Pentecostal Religious Experience." Unpublished doctor's dissertation, Boston University, 1975.

1312 May, F. William. "The Holy Spirit's Gift of Tongues," *Voice*, 42 (October 1963): 4-5.

1313 May, L. Carlyle. "A Survey of Glossolalia and Related Phenomenon in Non-Christian Religions," *American Anthropologist*, 58 (February 1956): 75-96.

1314 Mayeda, G. *Le langage de l'Evangile*. Privately published, 1948.

1315 Mayer, Marvin K. "The Behavior of Tongues," *Journal of the American Scientific Affiliation*, 23 (September 1971): 89-95.

1316 _____. "The Behavior of Tongues," in *Speaking in Tongues: Let's Talk about It*, Watson E. Mills, editor. Word Books, 1973. Pp. 112-27.

1317 Mead, Margaret. "Holy Ghost People," *American Anthropologist*, 70 (June 1968): 10-14.

1318 Meares, Ainslie. "Theories of Hypnosis," in *Hypnosis in Modern Medicine*, Jerome M. Schneck, editor. Charles C. Thomas, 1963.

1319 Meeking, Basil and John McTernan. "The Roman Catholic-Pentecostal Dialogue," *One in Christ*, 10 (1974): 106-16.

1320 Meeks, Fred E. "Pastor and the Tongues Movement," *Southwestern Journal of Theology*, 19 (Spring 1977): 73-85.

1321 _____. "Pastoral Care and Glossolalia: Implications of the Contemporary Tongues Movement in American Churches." Unpublished doctor's dissertation, Southwestern Baptist Theological Seminary, 1976.

1322 Mehl, Roger. "Approche sociologique des mouvements charismtiques," *Bulletin de la Société du Protestantisme Francais* (octobre-novembre-décembre 1974): 555-73.

1323 Meinhold, Peter. *Aussenseiter in den Kirchen*. Herder and Herder, 1977.

1324 Melançon, O. *Renouveau charismatique: Prophétisme, analyse théologique; Discernment des esprits, signes des temps.* Privately published, 1973.

1325 Meldau, Fred J. *the Fascinating Delusion of Pentecostalism.* Christian Victory Publishing Company, n.d.

1326 Melton, J. Gordon. *Catholic Pentecostal Movement: A Bibliography.* Institute for the Study of American Religion, 1976.

1327 Mensbrugghe, Françoise van der. *Les Mouvements de Renouveau Charismatique. Retour de l'Esprit? Retour de Dionysos?* Dissertation, Faculté Autonome de Théologie, Université de Genève, 1978.

1328 Menzies, William W. "The Non-Wesleyan Origins of the Pentecostal Movement," in *Aspects of Pentecostal-Charismatic Origins,* Vinson Synan, editor. Logos International, 1975. Pp. 81-98.

1329 Metz, Donald. *Speaking in Tongues: An Analysis.* Nazarene Publishing House, 1964.

1330 Meyer, Harding. "Die Pfingstbewegung in Brasilien," *Die evangelische Diaspora. Fahrbuch des Gustav-Adolf-Vereins,* 39 (1968): 9-50.

1331 Meyer, Johann A. G. *De charismatic praesertim Act. et 1 Cor. xiv.* Lamminger, 1797.

1332 Meyer, Matthew M. "Speaking in Tongues—Glossolalia," *Brethren Life and Thought,* 20 (1975): 133-50.

1333 Michael, John H. "The Gift of Tongues at Corinth," *The Expositor,* 4 (September 1907): 252-66.

1334 Michalon, P. "Témoignages et réglexions sur le mouvement catholique pentecostal," *Unité chrétienne,* 28 (November 1972): 60-70.

1335 _____. "Témoignages et réflexions sur un 'réveil' spirituel," *Unité chrètienne,* 34 (1974): 23-43.

1336 Miegge, Mario. "La diffusion du Protestantisme dans les zones sous-developpees de l'Italie meridionale," *Archives de sciences sociales des religions,* 4:8 (1959): 81-96.

1337 Miles, John. "Basic Bible Approach and Interpretation," *Voice,* 44 (March 1965): 8-9.

1338 _____. "The Basic Nature of Gifts," *Voice,* 44 (April 1965): 8-9.

1339 _____. "Spiritual Gifts and Christian Victory," *Voice,* 44 (May 1965): 8-9.

1340 _____. "Tongues," *Voice*, 44 (February 1965): 5-6.

1341 Miller, Irving R. "The Prophetic Meaning of Sectarian Ecstasy," *Religion in Life*, 17 (Winter 1947-1948): 104-11.

1342 Mills, Watson E. "Ecstaticism as a Background for Glossolalia," *Journal of the American Scientific Affiliation*, 27:4 (1975): 167-71.

1343 _____. "Glossolalia," in *Encyclopedia of Religion in the South*, Samuel S. Hill, editor. Mercer University Press, 1984. Pp. 305-306.

1344 _____. "Glossolalia: Christianity's Counterculture Amidst a Silent Majority," *Christian Century*, 89 (September 27, 1972): 949-51.

1345 _____. "Glossolalia: Creative Sound or Destructive Fury," *Home Missions*, 43 (August 1972): 8-13.

1346 _____. "Glossolalia: The New Language of Zion," *People*, (July 1973): 34-37.

1347 _____. "Glossolalia as a Socio-Psychological Experience," *Search*, 3 (Winter 1973): 46-53.

1348 _____. "Glossolalia: A Study of Origins." Unpublished paper presented at the national meeting of the Society of Biblical Literature, Atlanta, October 1971.

1349 _____. "Listening to the Glossolaliac: Going Beyond Words," *Western Recorder*, 145 (January 2, 1971): 10.

1350 _____. "Literature on Glossolalia," *Journal of the American Scientific Affiliation*, 26:4 (1974): 169-73.

1351 _____. "A New Lingo for Christendom?" *Home Missions*, 41 (June 1970): 28-29.

1352 _____. "Reassessing Glossolalia," *Christian Century*, 87 (October 14, 1970): 1217-19.

1353 _____. *Speaking in Tongues: A Classified Bibliography*. Society for Pentecostal Studies, 1974.

1354 _____, ed. *Speaking in Tongues: Let's Talk about It*. Word Books, 1973.

1355 _____. "The Strange New Language of Christendom," in *The Lure of the Occult*, Watson E. Mills and M. Thomas Starkes, editors. Home Mission Board of the Southern Baptist Convention, 1974. Pp. 73-82.

1356 _____. "A Theological Interpretation of Tongues in Acts and 1 Corinthians." Unpublished doctor's dissertation, Southern Baptist Theological Seminary, 1968.

1357 _____. "Tongue Speech: Revolution or Renewal," *The Student*, 50 (November 1970): 29-31.

1358 _____. *Understanding Speaking in Tongues*. Eerdmans, 1972.

1359 Mink, Paul. *Ich bin der Herr, dein Arzt! Betrachtungen über die Heilung durch den Glauben nach dem Wort Gottes*. Maranatha-Mission, n.d.

1360 _____. *Wird die Einheitskirche kommen?* Maranatha-Mission, n.d.

1361 Miyata, Mitsuo. "Die verkuendigung des evangeliums in der Japanischen Gellschaft," *Zeitschrift für evangelische Ethik*, 24 (April 1980): 130-43.

1362 Moellering, H. Armin. "Charismata Reexamined," *Concordia Journal*, 5:5 (September 1979): 178-83.

1363 Molenaar, D. G. *De doop met de Heilige Geest*. Kok, 1963.

1364 Mollat, Donatien. *L'expérience de l'Expirit-Saint selon le Nouveau Testament*. Editions du Feu Nouveau, 1973.

1365 _____. *L'expérience spirituelle*. Editions du Feu Nouveau, 1974.

1366 _____. *La révélation du Saint-Esprit chez saint Jean*. Privately published, 1971.

1367 _____. "The Role of Experience in the New Testament Teaching on Baptism and the Coming of the Holy Spirit," *One in Christ*, 10:2 (1974): 129-47.

1368 Möller, F. P. *Die apostoliese leer*. Evangelie Uitgewers, 1961.

1369 Monléon, A. M. de. "Le Renouveau charismatique aux États-Unis," *Vers l'unité chrétienne*, 227 (1970): 81-85. Also in *Cahiers sur l'oraison*, (Editions du Feu Nouveau) 122 (March-April 1972): 242-53.

1370 Montague, George T. "Baptism in the Spirit and Speaking in Tongues: A Biblical Appraisal," *Theology Digest*, 21 (1973): 342-60.

1371 _____. *The Holy Spirit: Growth of a Biblical Tradition*. Paulist Press, 1976.

1372 _____. *The Spirit and His Gifts: The Biblical Background of Spirit-Baptism, Tongue-Speaking and Prophecy*. Paulist Press, 1974.

1373 Moody, Dale. "Charismatic and Official Ministries," *Interpretation*, 19 (April 1965): 168-81.

1374 _____. "Speaking in Tongues," *Proclaim*, 9 (1979): 13.

1375 Moody, Jess C. *The Jesus Freaks*. Word Books, 1971.

1376 Moore, John. "The Catholic Pentcostal Movement," *Doctrine and Life*, 23 (April 1973): 177-96.

1377 Moorehead, William G. "Tongues of Fire," in *The International Standard Bible Encyclopedia*. 5 vols. The Howard-Severance Company, 1915. 5: 2997-98.

1378 Morentz, Paul. "Lecture on Glossolalia." Unpublished paper, University of California, 1966.

1379 Morgan, G. Campbell. *The Spirit of God*. Revell, 1900.

1380 Morgan, Jan. " 'Tongues' Gaining in Protestantism," *Louisville Courier Journal*, (June 24, 1964): 3.

1381 Morr, Harold Francis. "These Signs Shall Follow Them That Believe." Unpublished critical monograph, Grace Theological Seminary, 1953.

1382 Morris, Fred B. "Now I Want You All to Speak in Tongues," *The Christian Advocate*, 7 (July 4, 1963): 9-10.

1383 Morris, John Warren. "The Charismatic Movement: An Orthodox Evaluation," *Greek Orthodox Theological Review*, 28 (Summer 1983): 103-34.

1384 Mosiman, Edison. "A Dissertation on the Gift of Tongues in the New Testament." Unpublished master's thesis, University of Chicago, 1910.

1385 _____. *Das Zungenreden geschichtlich und psychologisch untersucht*. J. C. B. Mohr, 1911.

1386 Motley, Michael T. "Glossolalia: Analyses of Selected Aspects of Phonology and Morphology." Unpublished master's thesis, University of Texas, 1967.

1387 Mountain, J. *Authority, Demons and Tongues*. Privately published, n.d.

1388 Moura, Abdalazis de. *Importância das Igrejas Pentecostais para a Igreja Católica*. Duplicated typescript, de Moura, Rua Jirquiti 48, Boa Vista, 1969.

1389 Mouw, Richard. "Catholic Pentecostalism Today," *The Reformed Journal* (July-August): 8-15.

1390 Moyer, Harold S. "The Jesus Revolution," *Brethren Life and Thought*, 17:3 (1972): 169-74.

1391 Muelder, W. G. "From Sect to Church: Rural Pentecostal Sects and the Church of the Nazarene," *Christendom*, 10 (1945): 450-62.

1392 Mueller, Theodore. "A Linguistic Analysis of Glossolalia," *Concordia Theological Monthly*, 45:3 (July 1981): 186-91.

1393 Mühlen, Heribert. "The Charismatic Renewal as Experience," *The Holy Spirit and Power*, Doubleday and Company, 1975. Pp. 107-17.

1394 _____. *A Charismatic Theology*. Paulist Press, 1978.

1395 _____. *Erfahrung mit dem Heiligen Geist*. Grünewald Verlag, 1979.

1396 _____. "Gemeinsame Geist-Erfahrung: Hoffnung für die getrennten Kirchen," *Una Sancta*, 36:1 (1981): 20-32.

1397 Müller, Alexander. "Die internationale Pfingstbewegung," *Informationsblatt*, 8 (May 22, 1959): 157-61.

1398 Munk, Gerald W. "The Charismatic Experience in the Orthodox Tradition," *Theosis*, 1:7 (November 1978): 1-3.

1399 Munro, John K. "The New Testament Spiritual Gifts." Unpublished master's thesis, Dallas Theological Seminary, 1940.

1400 Murphy, Laurence. "Que faut-il penser du mouvement de Jésus?," *Documentation catholique*, 70:2 (1973): 75-76.

1401 _____. "The Jesus Movement: A Critique," *Catholic Mind*, 71 (1973): 4-7.

1402 Murray, Andrew. *The Full Blessing of Pentecost: The One Thing Needful*. Revell, 1908.

1403 Murray, James S. "What We Can Learn From the Pentecostal Churches," *Christianity Today*, 11 (June 9, 1967): 10-12.

1404 "My Experience of Speaking in Tongues," *Our Hope*, 33 (May 1927): 684-87.

1405 Myland, Wesley T. *The Latter Rain*. Privately published, n.d.

N

1406 Nash, David F. *"Tongues" in Perspective: What Say the Scriptures?* Epworth Press, 1967.

1407 Neely, B. F. *Bible Versus the Tongues Theory.* Nazarene Publishing House, n.d.

1408 Neff, H. Richard. "The Cultural Basis for Glossolalia in the Twentieth Century," in *Speaking in Tongues: Let's Talk about It*, Watson E. Mills, editor. Word Books, 1973. Pp. 26-35.

1409 Neighbor, R. E. *Talking in Tongues.* Gems of Gold Publishing Company, n.d.

1410 Neitz, Mary J. "Slain in the Spirit: Creating and Maintaining a Religious Social Reality," *Religious Education*, 78 (Summer 1983): 423-24.

1411 Nelson, Donald E. "The Jesus People Movement," *The Baptist Challenge*, 12 (September 1972): 1-5.

1412 Ness, Henry H. *The Baptism with the Holy Spirit—What Is It?* Evangelism Crusaders, Inc., n.d.

1413 _____. *Manifestations of the Spirit.* Privately printed, n.d.

1414 Ness, William H. "Glossolalia in the New Testament," *Concordia Theological Monthly*, 32 (April 1961): 221-23.

1415 Neth, Frederick G. *Charismatic Principles in the Church.* Unpublished bachelor's thesis, North Park Theological Seminary, 1961.

1416 Nevius, J. L. *Demon Possession and Allied Themes.* Revell, 1894.

1417 Newbigen, J. E. Lesslie. "Die Pfingstler und die Ökumenische Bewegung," *Ökumenische Rundschau*, 13:4 (1964): 323-26.

1418 Newbold, W. R. "Spirit Writing and 'Speaking with Tongues,' " *Popular Science Monthly*, 49 (1921): 508.

1419 Newell, Arlo F. *Receive the Holy Spirit.* Warner Press, 1978.

1420 Newell, J. Philip. "Scottish Intimations of Modern Pentecostalism: A. J. Scott and the 1830 Clydeside Charismatics," *Pneuma*, 4:2 (Fall 1982): 1-18.

1421 "New Interest in Glossolaly: United Presbyterian Church Authorized Study," *America*, 118 (June 8, 1968): 744.

1422 Newport, John P. "Speaking in Tongues," *Home Missions*, 36 (May 1965): 7-9, 21-26.

1423 _____. "Understanding, Evaluating and Learning From the Contemporary Glossolalia Movement," in *Tongues*, Luther B. Dyer, editor. LeRoi Publishers, 1971. Pp. 105-27.

1424 Nichol, John Thomas. *Pentecostalism*. Harper and Row, 1966.

1425 _____. "The Role of the Pentecostal Movement in American Church History," *The Gordon Review*, 2 (December 1956).

1426 Nickel, Thomas R. *The Shakarian Story*. Full Gospel Business Men's Fellowship International, 1964.

1427 Nida, Eugene A. "Glossolalia: A Case of Pseudo-Linguistic Structure." Unpublished paper delivered at the 39th annual meeting of the Linguistic Society of America, New York City, December 1964.

1428 _____. "Preliminary Report on Glossolalia." A paper presented at the Linguistic Society of America, New York, 1964.

1429 Niesz, Nancy L. and Earl J. Kronenberger. "Self-Actualization in Glossolalic and Non-Glossolalia Pentecostals," *Sociological Analysis*, 39 (Fall 1978): 250-56.

1430 Nixon, Robin. "Ecumenism, Models of the Church and Styles of Authority," *Churchman*, 91 (July 1977): 229-41.

1431 "No Noisy Gongs," *America*, 111 (1964): 173-74.

1432 Noorbergen, Rene. *Charisma of the Spirit in Search of a Supernatural Experience*. Pacific Press Publishing Association, 1973.

1433 Northcott, John E. *The Congregation in Crisis: A Contextual Approach to Managing Conflict Between Neo-Pentecostal Authoritarianism and Lutheranism*. United Theological Seminary, 1981.

1434 Northrup, Bernard E. *What You Should Know About . . . Tongues and Spiritual Gifts*. San Francisco Baptist Theological Seminary, n.d.

1435 Nouwen, Henri. "The Pentecostal Movement: Three Perspectives," *Scholastic*, 109 (April 21, 1967): 15-17, 32.

1436 Nunn, David O. *Manifestations of the Spirit: The Three Glorious Gifts of Utterance—Divine Kinds of Tongues, Interpretation of Tongues, Prophecy.* Bible Revival Evangelistic Association, n.d.

O

1437 Oates, Wayne E. "Ecstaticism." Unpublished seminar paper, Duke University, 1943.

1438 _____. "A Socio-Psychological Study of Glossolalia," in _Glossolalia: Tongues Speaking in Biblical, Historical, and Psychological Perspective_, Frank Stagg, E. Glenn Hinson, and Wayne E. Oates, editors. Abingdon Press, 1967. Pp. 76-99.

1439 Ockenga, Harold J. _The Holy Spirit and Tongues_. Boston Park Street Church, 1965.

1440 _____. _Power Through Pentecost_. Eerdmans, 1959.

1441 _____. _The Spirit of the Living God_. Revell, 1947.

1442 O'Connell, Daniel C. and Ernest T. Bryant. "Some Psychological Reflections on Glossolalia," _Review for Religious_, 31 (1972): 974-77.

1443 O'Connor, Edward D. "Baptism of the Spirit: Emotional Therapy?" _Ave Maria_, 106 (1967): 11-14.

1444 _____. "Charism and Institution," _American Ecclesiastical Review_, 168:8 (October 1974): 507-25.

1445 _____. "The Hidden Roots of the Charismatic Renewal in the Catholic Church," in _Aspects of Pentecostal-Charismatic Origins_, Vinson Synan, editor. Logos International, 1975. Pp. 169-91.

1446 _____. "The Holy Spirit, Christian Love, and Mysticism," in _Perspectives on Charismatic Renewal_, Edward D. O'Connor, editor. University of Notre Dame Press, 1975. Pp. 133-44.

1447 _____. "The Literature of the Catholic, Charismatic Renewal 1967-1975," in *Perspectives on Charismatic Renewal*, Edward D. O'Connor, editor. University of Notre Dame Press, 1975. Pp. 145-84.

1448 _____. "The New Theology of Charisms in the Church," *American Ecclesiastical Review*, 161 (September 1969): 145-59.

1449 _____. *Pentecost in the Catholic Church*. Dove Publications, 1970.

1450 _____. "Pentecost and Catholicism," *The Ecumenist*, 6 (July-August 1968): 161-64.

1451 _____. *Pentecost in the Modern World: The Charismatic Renewal Compared with Other Trends in the Church and the World Today*. Ave Maria Press, 1972.

1452 _____. *The Pentecostal Movement in the Catholic Church*. Ave Maria Press, 1971.

1453 _____. "To Roman Catholic Priests Enquiring about the Pentecostal Movement." Unpublished paper, 1970.

1454 Oesterreich, T. K. *Possession: Demonical and Other*. Trans. D. Ibberson. University Books, 1966.

1455 Office of the General Assembly. *The World of the Holy Spirit*. United Presbyterian Church U.S.A., 1970.

1456 O'Hanlon, Daniel J. "Pentecostals and Pope John's New Pentecost," *America*, 108 (May 4, 1963): 634-36.

1457 Oke, Norman R. *Facing the Tongues Issue*. Beacon Hill Press, 1973.

1458 Olila, James H. "Pentecostalism: The Dynamics of Recruitment in a Modern Socio-Religious Movement." Unpublished master's thesis, University of Minnesota, 1968.

1459 Oliphant, M. O. *The Life of Edward Irving*. Hurst & Blacketts, n.d.

1460 Oliver, Bernard John, Jr. "Some Newer Religious Groups in the U.S.: Twelve Case Studies." Unpublished doctor's dissertation, Yale University, 1946.

1461 Olson, William G. *The Charismatic Church*. Bethany, 1974.

1462 Oman, John D. "On 'Speaking in Tongues': A Psychological Analysis," *Pastoral Psychology*, 14 (December 1963): 48-51.

1463 O'Mara, Philip F. "Ecumenism in the Catholic Charismatic Renewal Movement," *Journal of Ecumenical Studies*, 17 (Fall 1980): 647-57.

1464 Opsahl, Paul D., ed. *The Holy Spirit in the Life of the Church: From Biblical Times to the Present*. Augsburg Publishing House, 1978.

1465 Orr, Willian W. *If You Speak with Tongues—Here Are the Rules*. Grace Gospel Fellowship, n.d.

1466 Orsini, Joseph E. *Hear My Confession*. Logos International, 1971.

1467 Osowski, F. "Pentecost and Pentecostals: A Happening," *Review for Religious*, 27 (November 1968): 1064-88.

1468 Osser, H. A., et al. "Glossolalic Speech from a Psycholinguistic Perspective," *Journal of Psycholinguistic Research*, 2 (1973): 9-19.

1469 Osteen, John H. "He Heard God Speak," *Baptists and the Baptism of the Holy Spirit*, (1963): 6-10.

1470 Osterberg, A. G. "Azusa's 50th Anniversary," *The Foursquare Magazine*, (October 1956): 16-18.

1471 Ostling, R. N. "Jesus People Revisited," *International Review of Mission*, 63 (April 1974): 232-37.

1472 Oudersluys, Richard C. "The Purpose of Spiritual Gifts," *Reformed Review*, 28 (Spring 1975): 212-22.

1473 Owen, John. *On the Holy Spirit*. 2 vols. Protestant Episcopal Book Society, 1862.

PQ

1474 Pace, Enzo. "Charismatics and the Political Presence of Catholics: The Italian Case," *Social Compass*, 25:1 (1978): 85-99.

1475 Pache, Rene. *The Person and Work of the Holy Spirit*. Moody Press, 1954.

1476 Packer, James. "Charismatic Renewal: Pointing to a Person and a Power," *Christianity Today*, 24 (March 7, 1980): 1620.

1477 _____. *God Has Spoken*. Hodder & Stoughton, 1965.

1478 _____. "Theological Reflections on the Charismatic Movement," *Churchman*, 94:1-2 (1980): 7-25, 108-25.

1479 Palma, Anthony D. "Glossolalia in the Light of the New Testament and Subsequent History." Unpublished bachelor's thesis, Biblical Seminary, New York, 1960.

1480 _____. "The Holy Spirit in the Corporate Life of the Pauline Congregation." Unpublished doctor's dissertation, Concordia Seminary, 1974.

1481 _____. "Tongues and Prophecy: A Comparative Study in Charismata." Unpublished master's thesis, Concordia Seminary, 1966.

1482 Palmer, Edwin H. *The Holy Spirit*. Presbyterian and Reformed Publishing Company, 1962.

1483 Palmer, Everett W. "Speaking in Tongues," *Christian Advocate*, 8 (October 22, 1964): 9-10.

1484 _____. *Statement on the Tongues Movement*. Privately published, 1961.

1485 Palmer, Gary. "Studies of Tension Reduction in Glossolalia." Unpublished paper, University of Minnesota, 1966.

1486 _____. "Trance." Paper presented at the annual meeting of the Central States, Anthropological Society, Chicago, April 1967.

1487 _____. "Trance and Dissociation: A Cross-Cultural Study in Psychophysiology." Unpublished master's thesis, University of Minnesota, 1966.

1488 Palms, Roger C. *The Jesus Kids*. The Judson Press, 1972.

1489 Panton, D. M. *Irvingism, Tongues, and the Gifts of the Holy Ghost*. Charles J. Thynne and Jarvis, n.d.

1490 Papa, Mary. "Pentecostals: Wave of the Future?" *National Catholic Reporter*, 4 (June 5, 1969): 1-2.

1491 _____. "People Having a Good Time Praying," *National Catholic Reporter*, 3:39 (1967): 1-10.

1492 *Paraclete: A Journal Concerning the Person and Work of the Holy Spirit*. Assemblies of God Publishing House, n.d.

1493 Paris, Arthur, E. *Black Pentecostalism: Southern Religion in an Urban World*. University of Massachusetts Press, 1982.

1494 Parkes, William. "Pentecostalism: Its History, Background and Recent Trends," *London Quarterly & Holborn Review*, 35 (1966): 147-53.

1495 Parnell, Christopher W. "Understanding Tongue-Speaking." A draft manuscript, Southern Baptist Seminary, n.d.

1496 Parratt, J. K. "The Rebaptism of the Ephesian Disciples," *Expository Times*, 79 (June 1968): 182-83.

1497 Parsons, Anne. "The Pentecostal Immigrants: A Study of an Ethnic Central City Church," *Journal for the Scientific Study of Religion*, 4 (1965): 182-97.

1498 Patterson, Bob E. "Catholic Pentecostals," in *Speaking in Tongues: Let's Talk about It*, Watson E. Mills, editor. Word Books, 1973. Pp. 94-111.

1499 Pattison, E. Mansell. "Behavioral Research on the Nature of Glossolalia," *Journal of the American Scientific Affiliation*, 20 (September 1968): 73-86.

1500 _____. "Ideological Support for the Marginal Middle Class: Faith Healing and Glossolalia," in *Religious Movements in Contemporary America*, Irving I. Zaretsky and Mark P. Leone, editors. Princeton University Press, 1974.

1501 _____. "Speaking in Tongues and About Tongues," *Christian Standard*, 98 (February 15, 1964): 1-2.

1502 Pattison, E. Mansell and Robert L. Casey. "Glossolalia: A Contemporary Mystical Experience," in *Clinical Psychiatry and Religion*, E. Mansell Pattison, editor. Little, Brown and Company, 1968. Pp. 133-48.

1503 _____. "Glossolalia: A Contemporary Mystical Experience," *International Psychiatry Clinics*, 5 (1969): 133-48.

1504 Paul, George Harold. "The Religious Frontier in Oklahoma: Dan T. Muse and The Pentecostal Holiness Church." Unpublished doctor's dissertation, University of Oklahoma, 1965.

1505 Paul, Jonathan, ed. *Verhandlungen der Gnadauer Pfingstkonfernz uber das Einwohnen des Heiligen Geistes, den Gehorsam des Glaubens und Gemeinschaftspfleg in Deutschland*. Deutsche Evangelische Verlag, 1894.

1506 Paulk, Earl P. *Your Pentecostal Neighbour*. Pathway Press, 1958.

1507 Pavelsky, Robert Lee. "The Psychological Correlates of Act and Process Glossolalia as a Function of Socioeconomic Class, Expectation of Glossolalia and Frequency of Glossolalia Utterance." Unpublished doctor's dissertation, Fuller Theological Seminary, 1975.

1508 Pearlman, Myer. *The Heavenly Gift. Studies in the Work of the Holy Spirit*. Gospel Publishing House, 1935.

1509 Peck, Royal L. "Catholic Charismatics: The View from Italy," *Christianity Today*, 19 (June 20, 1975): 34.

1510 Pederson, Duane. *Jesus People*. Compass Press, 1972.

1511 _____. *This We Believe* . . . Pentecostal Church of God of America, n.d.

1512 Pelletier, Joseph. *A New Pentecost: Renewal in the Holy Spirit*. Assumption Publications, 1973.

1513 _____. "The Pentecostal Renewal," *Liguorian*, 59 (August 1971): 27-29.

1514 Pentecostal Church of God of America. General Constitution and By-Laws. N.p., 1966.

1515 Pentecostal Free Will Baptist Church. *Faith and Government of the Free Will Baptist Church of the Pentecostal Faith*. N.p., 1961.

1516 "Pentecostal Tongues and Converts," *Time*, 90 (July 28, 1967): 64.

1517 Perkins, David W. "Superspirituality in Corinth," *The Theological Educator*, 14:1 (Fall 1983): 41-52.

1518 Perkins, Jonathan E. *The Baptism of the Holy Spirit: An Explanation in Speaking in Other Languages as the Spirit Giveth Utterance.* B. N. Robertson Co., 1945.

1519 Perrin, Steven W. "A Clanging Cymbal: Conflict Among Catholic Pentecostals." Unpublished doctor's dissertation, University of Michigan State, 1971.

1520 "The Person and Work of the Holy Spirit, with Special Reference to 'the Baptism in the Holy Spirit.' " Report to the Presbyterian Church in the U.S., submitted to the General Assembly, 1971.

1521 Peyrot, Giorgio. *La circolare Buffarini-Guidi e i Pentecostali*, (Attuare la costituzione 26). Rome: Associazione Italiana per la Libertà della Cultura, 1955.

1522 Pfister, Oskar. "Die psychologische Enträtselung der Religiösen Glossolalie und der automatischen Kryptographie," *Jahrbuch für psychoanalytische und psychopathologische Forschungen*, 3 (1912): 427ff.

1523 Pfitzner, Victor. *Led in the Spirit.* Lutheran Publishing House, 1976.

1524 _____. "Office and Charism in Paul and Luke," *Colloquium*, 13 (May 81): 28-38.

1525 Philips, G. *De Spiritu Sancto et Ecclesia in theologia contemporanea (Cursus XVI).* Louvain University, 1957-58.

1526 Phillips, McCandlish. "And There Appeared to Them Tongues of Fire," *The Saturday Evening Post*, (May 16, 1964): 31-33, 39-40.

1527 Phillipson, John S. "Two Pentecostal Experiences," *America*, 121 (March 29, 1969): 360-63.

1528 Pickell, D. "Speaking in Tongues," *Cross and Crown*, 24 (Summer 1972): 280-85.

1529 Pierce, Flora M. Johnson. "Glossolalia," *Journal of Religion and Psychical Research*, 4 (July-October 1981): 168-78.

1530 Pierson, Arthur T. *Acts of the Holy Spirit.* Revell, 1896.

1531 _____. *Speaking with Tongues.* Gospel Publishing House, n.d.

1532 _____. "Speaking with Tongues," *Missionary Review*, 20 (1907): 487, 682.

1533 _____. "Speaking with Tongues," *Our Hope*, 14 (July 1907): 35-42.

1534 Pike, J. "Glossolalia," *The Living Church*, 146 (1963): 11.

1535 _____. "Pastoral Letter Regarding 'Speaking in Tongues,' "
Pastoral Psychology, 15 (May 1964): 56-61.

1536 Pikell, Donald E. "An Inside Look at Charismatic Catholics," *Liguorian*, 60 (September 1972): 46-49.

1537 _____. "Speaking in Tongues," *Cross and Crown*, 24 (September 1972): 280-85.

1538 Pilkington, G. *The Unknown Tongues Discovered to Be English, Spanish, and Latin; the Rev. Edward Irving Proved to be Erroneous in Attributing Their Utterance to the Influence of the Holy Spirit*. Privately published, 1831.

1539 Pin, Émile Jean. "En guise d'introduction, ou comment se sauver de l'anomie et de l'aliénation: Jesus People et Catholiques Pentecostaux," *Social Compass*, 21 (1974): 227-39.

1540 Pink, Arthur W. *The Holy Spirit*. Baker Book House, 1970.

1541 Pinnock, Clark H. "Charismatic Renewal for the Radical Church," *Post American*, 4 (Fall 1975): 16-21.

1542 _____. "The New Pentecostalism: Reflections of an Evangelical Observer," in *Perspectives on the New Pentecostalism*, Russell F. Spittler, editor. Baker Book House, 1976. Pp. 182-92.

1543 _____. "Opening the Church to the Charismatic Dimension," *Christianity Today*, 25 (June 12, 1981): 16.

1544 _____. "A Theological Evaluation and Critique," in *Tongues*, Luther B. Dyer, editor. LeRoi Publishers, 1971. Pp. 128-41.

1545 Pinnock, Clark H. and Grant R. Osborne. "A Truce Proposal for the Tongues Controversy," *Christianity Today*, 16 (October 8, 1971): 6-9.

1546 Pitts, John, et. al. "Spiritual Healing," *Religion in Life*, 25 (Spring 1956): 163-204.

1547 Plog, Stanley C. "Preliminary Analysis of Group Questionnaires on Glossolalia." Unpublished data, University of California, 1966.

1548 _____. "UCLA Conducts Research on Glossolalia," *Trinity*, 3 (1964): 38-39.

1549 Plowman, Edward E. "Catholic Charismatics: An Evangelistic Thrust," *Christianity Today*, 22 (September 22, 1978): 42.

1550 _____. "Deepening Rift in the Charismatic Movement," *Christianity Today*, 20 (October 10, 1975): 52-54.

1551 _____. *The Jesus Movement: Accounts of Christian Revolutionaries in Action*. Hodder & Stoughton, 1972.

1552 Plumptre, Edward H. "Tongues, Confusion of," in *Smith's Dictionary of the Bible*, H. B. Hackett, editor. 4 vols. Houghton, Mifflin and Company, 1892-1896. 4: 3285-304.

1553 _____. "Tongues, Gift of," in *Smith's Dictionary of the Bible*, H. B. Hackett, editor. 4 vols. Houghton, Mifflin and Company, 1892-1896. 4: 3305-12.

1554 Pollock, A. J. *Modern Pentecostalism, Foursquare Gospel, Healings and Tongues*. The Central Bible Truth Depot, n.d.

1555 Poloma, Margaret M. *The Charismatic Movement: Is There a New Pentecost?* Twayne, 1982.

1556 _____. "Christian Covenant Communities: An Adaptation of the International Community for Urban Life," in *A Reader in Sociology: A Christian Perspective*, Charles DeSanto, et al., editors. Herald Press, 1980. Pp. 609-30.

1557 _____. "Toward a Christian Sociological Perspective: Religious Values, Theory, and Methodology," *Sociological Analysis*, 43 (Summer 1982): 95-108.

1558 Polovina, Samuel Emil. "Light on the Tongues Movement," *Herald of Holiness*, 5 (December 13, 1916): 8.

1559 Pope, R. Martin. "Gift of Tongues," in *A Dictionary of the Apostolic Church*, James Hastings, editor. 2 vols. Scribner's Sons, 1908. 1: 598-99.

1560 _____. "The Holy Spirit," *Lexington Theological Quarterly*, 15 (July 1980): 82-96.

1561 Powers, James F. "Catholic Pentecostals," *America*, 120 (July 20, 1963): 43-44.

1562 Poythress, Vern S. "Linguistic and Sociological Analyses of Modern Tongues-Speaking: Their Contributions and Limitations," *Westminster Theological Journal*, 42:2 (1980): 367-88.

1563 _____. "The Nature of Corinthian Glossolalia: Possible Options," *Westminster Theological Journal*, 40:1 (1977): 130-35.

1564 Pratt, James B. *The Religious Consciousness: A Psychological Study*. Macmillan and Company, 1945.

1565 "Preliminary Report." Unpublished paper, Division of Pastoral Services of the Episcopal Diocese of California, Study Commission of Glossolalia, 1963.

1566 Preus, Klemet. "Tongues: An Evaluation From a Scientific Perspective," *Concordia Theological Quarterly*, 46:4 (October 1982): 277-93.

1567 Price, Leslie. "What is Meant by Testing the Spirits," *Journal of the Academy of Religion and Psychical Research*, 3 (July 1980): 210-13.

1568 Pridie, J. R. *The Spiritual Gifts*. Robert Scott, 1921.

1569 Priebe, Duane Allen. "Charismatic Gifts and Christian Existence in Paul," in *Gifts of the Spirit and the Body of Christ*, J. Elmo Agrimson, editor. Augsburg, 1974. Pp. 15-33.

1570 Prince, Raymond. "Sociolinguistic vs. Neurophysiological Explanations for Glossolalia: Comment on Goodman's Paper," *Journal for the Scientific Study of Religion*, 11 (1972): 293-96.

1571 _____, ed. *Trance and Possession States*. R. M. Bucke Memorial Society, 1968.

1572 Prokhanoff, Haralan. *In the Cauldron of Russia*. John Felsberg, 1933.

1573 "Protestant Episcopal Church in the U.S.A. Diocese of California." Division of Pastoral Services, Study Commission on Glossolalia, May 1963.

1574 Pruitt, Lawrence D. *Modern Pentecostalism*. Faith Publishing House, n.d.

1575 Pulkingham, W. G. *Gathered for Power: Charisma, Communalism, Christian Witness*. Morehouse-Barlow, 1972.

1576 Purkiser, Westlake T. *Conflicting Concepts of Holiness: Some Current Issues in the Doctrine of Sanctification*. Beacon Hill Press, 1953.

1577 _____. *The Gifts of the Spirit*. Beacon Hill Press, 1975.

1578 Putnam, W. G. "Tongues, Gift of," in *New Bible Dictionary*, J. D. Douglas, editor. Eerdmans, 1962. Pp. 1286-87.

1579 Pyle, Hugh F. *Truth about Tongues*. Accent Books, 1976.

1580 Quebedeaux, Richard. *The New Charismatics: The Origins, Development and Significance of Neo-Pentecostalism*. Doubleday and Company, 1976.

1581 _____. *The New Charismatics II*. Harper and Row, 1983.

1582 _____. *The Worldly Evangelicals*. Harper and Row, 1978.

R

1583 Radano, John H. "Response to P. O'Mara's 'Ecumenism in the Catholic Charismatic Renewal Movement,' " *Journal of Ecumenical Studies*, 17 (Fall 1980): 657-60.

1584 Radford, William F. *Apostolic Teaching Concerning Tongues*. Pentecostal Nazarene Publishing House, n.d.

1585 Ramm, Bernard. *A Study of Some Special Problems in Reference to the Speaking in Tongues*. Bible Institute of Los Angeles, 1947.

1586 _____. *The Witness of the Spirit*. Eerdmans, 1960.

1587 Ramsey, Michael, et al. "Life in the Spirit: Lectures Read at a Conference for Anglican Religious at St. John's College," York, 1974.

1588 Ranaghan, Kevin. "Catholic Charismatic Renewal: The First Seven Years," in *The Spirit and the Church*, Ralph Martin, editor. Paulist Press, 1976. Pp. 56-65.

1589 _____. *The Lord, the Spirit, and the Church*. Charismatic Renewal Services, 1973.

1590 _____. "Origins and Growth of the Charismatic Renewal," *Tablet*, 226 (September 2, 1972): 828-29.

1591 _____. "The Word on Speaking in Tongues," *National Catholic Reporter*, 3 (April 26, 1967): 4.

1592 Ranaghan, Kevin. *As the Spirit Leads Us*. Paulist-Neuman Press, 1971.

1593 Ranaghan, Kevin and Dorothy Ranaghan, eds. *Catholic Pentecostals*. Paulist-Neuman Press, 1969.

1594 Randall, J. *In God's Providence: The Birth of a Catholic Charismatic Parish*. Logos International, 1973.

1595 ————. "J'ai reçu le Baptême de l'Esprit," *Expériences*, 2 (1971): 11-12.

1596 Rarick, William John. "The Socio-Cultural Context of Glossolalia: A Comparison of Pentecostal and Neo-Pentecostal Religious Attitudes and Behavior." Unpublished doctor's dissertation, Fuller Theological Seminary, 1982.

1597 Raskopf, R. W. "Recent Literature on the Pentecostal Movement," *Anglican Theological Review*, sup. ser. 2 (1973): 113-18.

1598 "Rector and a Rumpus," *Newsweek*, 56 (July 4, 1960): 77.

1599 Reed, David A. "Aspects of the Origins of Oneness Pentecostalism," in *Aspects of Pentecostal-Charismatic Origins*, Vinson Synan, editor. Logos International, 1975. Pp. 143-68.

1600 ————. "Pentecostalism and the Ecumenical Movement Since 1948." Unpublished paper, Andover Newton Theological School, 1969.

1601 Regimbal, J. P. "Le renouveau charismatique dans l'Église catholique: Interview avec L. Coutu," *Orient*, 21:122 (1973) 112-15.

1602 ————. *Signes et témoins du Royaume 1: Sous la mouvance de l'Esprit: Le renouveau charismatique dans l'Église catholique*. Ralliement pour le Christ, 1971.

1603 Reid, Samuel Joseph. *What Saith the Scriptures: Concerning Healing of the Body, "Tongues," Baptism of the Holy Spirit*. Privately published, n.d.

1604 Reilly, T. à K. "The Gift of Tongues: What Was It?" *American Ecclesiastical Review*, 43 (July-December 1910): 3-25.

1605 ————. "Tongues," *Catholic Encyclopedia*, 14 (1912): 776-77.

1606 Reiser, Werner, et al. *Industrielle Sonntagsarbeit*. Flamberg-Verlag, 1960.

1607 Remy, Jean and J. P. Hiernaux. "Charismatic and Socio-Political Movements," *Social Compass*, 25:1 (1978): 7-163.

1608 "Report of the Committee on Spiritual Gifts." Reports and Actions of the Second General Convention of the American Lutheran Church, 1964.

1609 "Report of the Field Study Committee on Speaking in Tongues." Commission on Evangelism of the American Lutheran Church, 1972.

1610 "Report on Glossolalia." A report of the Commission on Evangelism of the American Lutheran Church, Minneapolis, 1962.

1611 "Report of the Special Commission on Glossolalia." To the Right Reverend Gerald Francis Burrill, Bishop of Chicago, December 12, 1960.

1612 "Report of the Special Committee on the Work of the Holy Spirit." A report of the United Presbyterian Church of the U.S.A., Philadelphia, 1970.

1613 Reuber, Kurt. *Mystik in der Gemeinschaftsfrömmigkeit der Heilegungsbewegung*. Gütersloh, 1938.

1614 Reuss, Ed. "La glossolalie: Chapitre de psychologie évangélique," *Revue théologique de Strasbourg*, 3 (1851): 65-97.

1615 von de Reuter, F. *Psychical Experiences of a Musician*. Simpkin, Marshall, Hamilton, Kent, 1928.

1616 Rhode, E. *Psyche, Seelencult U. Unsterblichkeitsglaube Der Griechten*. J. C. B. Mohr, 1921.

1617 Ribeiro, De Oliveira Pedro A. "Renouveau Charismatique au Bresil," *Social Compass*, 25:1 (1978): 37-42.

1618 Rice, John R. *The Charismatic Movement*. Sword of the Lord Publishers, 1976.

1619 _____. *The Power of Pentecost*. Sword of the Lord Publishers, 1949.

1620 _____. "Should One Talk in Tongues to Edify Self?" *The Sword of the Lord*, (September 19, 1952): 2.

1621 _____. *Speaking with Tongues*. Sword of the Lord Publishers, 1970.

1622 _____. "Speaking with Tongues," in *The Power of Pentecost*. Sword of the Lord Publishers, 1949. Pp. 203-76.

1623 Rice, Robert. "Charismatic Revival," *Christian Life*, 25 (November 1963): 30-32.

1624 _____. "Charismatic Revival," *View*, 2:1 (1965): 12-16, 22.

1625 _____. "Christian Glossolalia Through the Centuries," *View*, 1 (1964): 1-7.

1626 Rich, Arthur. *Christliche Existenz in der industriellen Welt*. Zwingli-Verlag, 1957.

1627 _____. *Die Weltlichkeit des Glaubens. Diakonie im Horizont der Säkularisierung*. Zwingli-Verlag, 1966.

1628 Richards, W. T. H. *Pentecost Is Dynamite*. Abingdon Press, 1974.

1629 Richardson, James T. "Psychological Interpretations of Glossolalia: A Reexamination of Research," *Journal for the Scientific Study of Religion*, 12 (1973): 199-207.

1630 Richardson, James T. and M. T. V. Reidy. "Form and Fluidity into Contemporary Glossolalic Movements," *The Annual Reivew of the Social Sciences of Religion*, 4 (1980): 183-220.

1631 Richardson, Richard A. "I Fought It, Then I Sought It," *Voice*, 11 (December 1963): 18-20.

1632 Richardson, Robert P. "Pentecostal Prophets," *Open Court*, 42 (1928): 673-80.

1633 Richet, Charles. "Xenoglossie: l'ecriture automatique en langues etrangeres," *Proceedings of the Society for Psychical Research*, 19 (1905-1907): 162-94.

1634 Richstätter, K. "Die Glossolalie im Lichte der Mystik," *Scholastik*, 2 (1936): 321-45.

1635 Ridout, George W. *The Deadly Fallacy of Spurious Tongues*. Pentecostal Publishing House, n.d.

1636 _____. *Spiritual Gifts, Including the Gift of Tongues: A Consideration of the Gifts of the Spirit and Particularly the Gift of Tongues, the "Pneumatika" and the "Charismata of 1 Corinthians."* Nazarene Publishing House, n.d.

1637 Riedel, Warren C. "A Biblical Approach to the Gifts of the Holy Spirit." Unpublished master's thesis, Lancaster Theological Seminary, 1971.

1638 Rifkin, Jeremy. *The Emerging Order: God in the Age of Scarcity*. G. P. Putnam's Sons, 1979.

1639 Rigaux, B. "L'anticipation du salut eschatologique par l' Esprit," *Analecta Biblica*, 42 (1969): 101-35.

1640 Rigby, Christopher. "A Personal Report on Catholic Pentecostalism," *The Ecumenist*, 7 (July-August 1969): 73-76.

1641 Riggs, Ralph M. *The Spirit Himself*. Gospel Publishing House, 1949.

1642 Righter, James D. "A Critical Study of the Charismatic Experience of Speaking in Tongues." Unpublished doctor's dissertation, Wesley Theological Seminary, 1974.

1643 Riley, William B. *Speaking with Tongues*. Privately published, n.d.

1644 Riocreux, Jean-Yves. "Réflexions d'un Franqis aux Etats-Unis," *La Vie Spirituelle*, 128 (January-February 1974): 23-30.

1645 Riss, Richard. "The Latter Rain Movement of 1948," *Pneuma*, 4:1 (Spring 1982): 32-45.

1646 Ritter, Adolf Martin. *Charisma im Verstandis des Joannes Chrysostomos und seiner Zeit*. Vandenhoeck & Ruprecht, 1972.

1647 Ritter, Adolf Martin and Gottfried Leich. *Wer ist die Kirche? Amt und Gemeinde im Neuen Testament, in der Kirchengeschichte und heute*. Vandenhoeck & Ruprecht, 1968.

1648 R. M. Bucke Memorial Society. *Personality Change and Religious Experience: Proceedings of the First Annual Conference*. Privately published, 1965.

1649 Robeck, Cecil M. "Written Prophecies: A Question of Authority (Protestant and Roman Catholic Charismatics)," *Pneuma*, 2:2 (Fall 1980): 26-45.

1650 Roberts, Oral. *The Baptism with the Holy Spirit and the Value of Speaking in Tongues Today*. Privately puiblished, 1964.

1651 _____. *The Call: Oral Roberts' Autobiography*. Doubleday and Company, 1972.

1652 Roberts, Peter. "A Sign—Christian or Pagan [1 Corinthians 14:21-25]?" *Expository Times*, 90 (April 1979): 199-203.

1653 Robertson, Carl F. "The Nature of New Testament Glossolalia." Unpublished doctor's dissertation, Dallas Theological Seminary, 1975.

1654 Robertson, O. Palmer. "Tongues: Sign of Covenantal Curse and Blessing," *Westminster Theological Journal*, 38:53 (1975): 43-53.

1655 Robinson, Donald W. "Charismata vs. Pneumatika: Paul's Method of Discussion," *Reformed Theological Review*, 31 (May-August 1972): 49-55.

1656 Robinson, Douglas. "The Ordo Salutis and Charismatic Movement," *Churchman*, 97:3 (1983): 232-43.

1657 Robinson, Wayne A. *I Once Spoke in Tongues*. Forum House Publishers, 1973.

1658 Roddy, Andrew Jackson. *Though I Spoke with Tongues: A Personal Testimony*. The Harvester, 1952.

1659 Rodriguez, Sylvia B. "Ecstasy: Map and Threshold, A Cross-Cultural Study of Dissociation." Unpublished doctor's dissertation, Stanford University, 1981.

1660 Roe, Norman D. "Aggression and Charismatics," *Theology Today*, 35 (April 1978): 81-83.

1661 Roebling, Karl. *Pentecostals Around the World*. Exposition Press, 1978.

1662 Roehrs, Stephen Paul. "Glossolalia Phenomena." Unpublished master's thesis, Concordia Theological Seminary, 1971.

1663 Rogers, Cleon L. "The Gift of Tongues in the Post Apostolic Church," *Bibliotheca Sacra*, 122 (April-June 1965): 134-43.

1664 Rogge, Louis. "Catholic Pentecostalism," *Sword*, 32:1 (February 1972): 6-23.

1665 _____. "Ecumenical Aspects of Catholic Pentecostalism," *Sword*, 32:2 (June 1972): 11-24.

1666 _____. "The Woman Named Mary," *Pneuma*, 4:2 (Fall 1982): 19-32.

1667 Rolim, Francisco C. "Pentecotisme et Societe au Bresil," *Social Compass*, 26:203 (1979): 345-72.

1668 _____. *Religão e classes populares*. Vozes, 1980.

1669 Rooth, Richard Arlen. "Social Structure in a Pentecostal Church." Unpublished master's thesis, University of Minnesota, 1967.

1670 Rose, Delbert Roy. "Distinguishing Things that Differ," *Wesleyan Theological Journal*, 9 (Spring 1974): 5-14.

1671 Ross, Brian. "James Eustace Purdie: The Story of Pentecostal Theological Education," *Journal of the Canadian Church Historical Society*, 17 (December 1975): 94-103.

1672 _____. "Donald Gee: Sectarian in Search of a Church," *The Evangelical Quarterly*, 50 (April-June 1978): 94-103.

1673 Roth, Richard A. "Recruitment and Organization in a Racially Mixed Pentecostal Church." Paper read at the annual meeting of the Central States Anthropological Society, University of Chicago, April 1967.

1674 Rowe, Michael. "Pentecostal Documents from the USSR," *Religion in Communist Lands*, 3 (January-June 1975): 25-30.

1675 _____. "Soviet Pentecostals: Movement for Emigration," *Religion in Communist Lands*, 5 (Autumn 1977): 170-74.

1676 Ruble, Richard Lee. "A Spiritual Evaluation of Tongues in Contemporary Theology." Unpublished doctor's dissertation, Dallas Theological Seminary, 1964.

1677 Runia, K. "The Forms and Functions of Nonsense Language," *Linguistics*, 50 (1969): 70-74.

1678 _____. "Glossolalia as Learned Behavior," *Canadian Journal of Theology*, 15 (1969): 60-64.

1679 _____. "Speaking in Tongues in the New Testament," *Vox Reformata*, (May 1965): 20-29, 38-46.

1680 Runyon, Theodore. *What the Spirit is Saying to the Churches*, Hawthorne Books, 1975.

1681 Rust, Hans. *Das Zungenreden*. Bergmann, 1924.

1682 _____. *Das Zungenreden: Eine Studie zur kritischen Religionspsychologie*. Bergmann, 1923.

1683 Ruth, Christian W. "The Gift of Tongues," *Herald of Holiness*, 13 (December 24, 1924): 4-5.

1684 Ryan, Herbert J. "Episcopalians, Pentecostalism and the Anglican Tradition," *St. Luke's Journal of Theology*, 18 (March 1975): 123-49.

1685 Ryan, John. *The Jesus People*. Sheed and Ward, Ltd., 1972.

1686 Rylaarsdam, J. C. "Pentecost," in *The Interpreter's Dictionary of the Bible*, George Arthur Buttrick, editor. 4 vols. Abingdon Press, 1962. K-Q: 727.

1687 Ryrie, Charles C. *The Holy Spirit*. Moody Press, n.d.

1688 _____. "The Significance of Pentecost," *Bibliotheca Sacra*, 112 (October 1955): 330-39.

S

1689 Saake, H. "Paulus als Ekstatiker: Pneumatologische Beobachtungen zu 2 Kor. 12:1-10," *Biblica*, 53:3 (1972): 404-10.

1690 Sabatier, A. "Glossolalie," in *Encyclopédie des Sciences Religieuses*. F. Lichtenberger, editor. 13 vols. Librairie Sanduz et Fischbacher, 1878. 5: 602-605.

1691 Sadler, A. W. "Glossolalia and Possession: An Appeal to the Episcopal Study Commission," *Journal for the Scientific Study of Religion*, 4 (1964): 84-90.

1692 Sala, Harold J. "An Investigation of the Baptizing and Filling Work of the Holy Spirit in the New Testament Related to the Pentecostal Doctrine of 'Internal Evidence.' " Unpublished doctor's dissertation, Bob Jones University, 1966.

1693 Salazar, Jose V. "La renovacion carismatica y su proyeccion social en la union zacapa: un municipio que hace honor a su nombre," *Estudios Teologicos*, 7 (July-December 1980): 215-34.

1694 Samarin, William J. "Book review of Goodman's *Speaking in Tongues*," *Language*, 50 (1974): 207-12.

1695 _____. "Book review of Kildahl's *The Psychology of Speaking in Tongues*," *Journal of Psycholinguistic Research*, 2 (1973): 171-74.

1696 _____. "Book review of Kildahl's *The Psychology of Speaking in Tongues*," *Sisters Today*, 44 (August-September 1972): 42-43.

1697 _____. "Evolution in Glossolalic Private Language," *Anthropological Linguistics*, 13 (1971): 55-67.

1698 _____. *The Forgotten Father*. Hodder & Stoughton, 1980.

1699 _____. "Forms and Functions of Nonsense Language," *Linguistics*, 50 (July 1969): 70-74.

1700 _____. "Glossolalia," *Psychology Today*, (August 1972): 48.

1701 _____. "Glossolalia as Learned Behavior," *Canadian Journal of Theology*, 15 (1969): 60-64.

1702 _____. "Glossolalia as Learned Behavior." Unpublished paper presented to annual meeting of the Society for Scientific Study of Religion, Montreal, 1968.

1703 _____. "Glossolalia as Regressive Speech," *Language and Speech*, 16 (1973): 77-89.

1704 _____. "Glossolalia as Regressive Speech." Unpublished paper presented at the meeting of the Linguistic Society of America, Columbus, Ohio, 1970.

1705 _____. "Glossolalia as a Vocal Phenomenon," in *Speaking in Tongues: Let's Talk about It*, Watson E. Mills, editor. Word Books, 1973. Pp. 128-42.

1706 _____. "The Glossolalist's 'Grammar of Use.'" Paper given at the annual meeting of the American Anthropological Association, San Diego, 1970.

1707 _____. "The Language of Religion." A paper presented at the annual meeting of the Society for the Scientific Study of Religion, Chicago, 1971.

1708 _____. "Language in Resocialization," *Practical Anthropology*, 17 (1970): 269-79.

1709 _____. "The Linguisticality of Glossolalia," *The Hartford Quarterly*, 8 (1968): 49-75.

1710 _____. "Religious Goals of a Neo-Pentecostal Group in a Non-Pentecostal Church," in *Perspectives on the New Pentecostalism*, Russell F. Spittler, editor. Baker Book House, 1976. Pp. 134-49.

1711 _____. "Sociolinguistic versus Neurophysiological Explanations for Glossolalia," *Journal for the Scientific Study of Religion*, 11 (Spring 1972): 293-99.

1712 _____. "Theory of Order with Disorderly Data." Paper presented at the Symposium on the Relation of Anthropology to Linguistics at the Annual Meeting of the American Anthropological Association, New York, 1971.

1713 _____. *Tongues of Men and Angels: The Religious Language of Pentecostalism*. Macmillan and Company, 1972.

1714 _____. "Variation and Variables in Religious Glossolalia," in *Language and Society*, Dell Haymes, editor. Cambridge University Press, 1972. Pp. 121-30.

1715 _____. "Worship in Sign Language," *Acts*, 1:4 (1968): 27-28.

1716 Sanders, J. Oswald. *The Holy Spirit and His Gifts*. Zondervan, 1970.

1717 Sandidge, Jerry L. "The Origin and Development of the Catholic Charismatic Movement in Belgium," Catholic University of Leuven, 1976.

1718 _____. "A Pentecostal Response to Roman Catholic Teaching on Mary," *Pneuma*, 4:2 (Fall 1982): 33-42.

1719 Santos, Geraldino dos. "Diversidade e intergração dos grupos pentecostais," in *O Espírto Santo*. ASTE, 1966. Pp. 30-32.

1720 Sargant, William. *The Mind Possessed: A Physiology of Possession, Mysticism and Faith Healing*. Penguin, 1974.

1721 _____. "Some Critical Group Abreactive Techniques and Their Relation to Modern Treatments," *Proceedings of the Royal Society of Medicine*, 92 (May 1949): 367-74.

1722 Sartori, Luigi. "The Structure of Juridical and Charismatic Power in the Christian Community," *Charisms in the Church*, Christian Duquoc and Casiano Floristan, editors. The Seabury Press, 1978. Pp. 56-66.

1723 Sassaman, Marcus B. "An Investigation of the Interpretations of Glossolalia." Unpublished bachelor's thesis, Western Evangelical Seminary, 1966.

1724 Satre, Lowell J. "Glossolalia in the New Testament," *Reports and Actions of the Second General Convention of the American Lutheran Church*, 1964.

1725 Saxman, John H. "Schizophrenic Speech: Selected Fundamental and Rate Characteristics." Unpublished doctor's dissertation, Purdue University, 1965.

1726 Scaer, David P. "The Charismatic Movement as Ecumenical Phenomenon," *Concordia Theological Quarterly*, 45 (January-April 1981): 81-83.

1727 _____. "An Essay for Lutheran Pastors on the Charismatic Movement," *The Springfielder*, 37 (1974): 210-23.

1728 Scaramelli, G. B. *Direttorio mistico*. N.p., 1754.

1729 Schafer, Rolf. *Der Evangelische Glaube*. J. C. B. Mohr, 1973.

1730 Schat, J. H. *Spreken met andere tongen*. Pinkster-Kergenootschap, 1963.

1731 Schjelderup, Harald K. "Psychologische Analyse eines Falles von Zungenreden," *Zeitschrift für Psychologie*, 122 (1931): 1-27.

1732 Schlauch, Margaret. *The Gift of Tongues*. Modern Age Books, 1942.

1733 Schlosser, Katesa. *Eingeborenenkirchen in Süd- und Südwestafrika, ihre Geschichte und Sozialstruktur. Erlebnisse einer völkerkundlichen Studienreise*. Walter, 1953.

1734 _____. "Profane Urschen des anschlusses an Separatistenkirchen in Süd- und Südwestafrika," in *Messianische Kirchen*, E. Benz, editor. E. J. Brill, 1967. Pp. 25-45.

1735 Schmidt, Karl L. "Das Penuma Hagion als Person und als Charisma," *Eranos Jahrbuch*, 13 (1965): 187-231.

1736 _____. *Die pfingsterzahlung und das pfingstereignis*. J. C. Hinrichs, 1919.

1737 Schmidt, Ludwig. "Koenig und charisma im alten testament: beobachtungen zur struktur des koenigtums in alten Israel," *Kerygma und Dogma*, 28 (January-March 1982): 73-87.

1738 Schmidt, Wolfgang. *Die Pfingstbewegung in Finnland*. Kirchengeschichtliche Gesellschaft Finnlands, 1935.

1739 Schmitz, D. O. *Die Bedeutung der urchristlichen Geistesgaben für unsere Zeit*. Offprint of the Nachrichtendienst der Pressestelle der Evangelischen Kirche der Rheinprovince, 3:4 (1949).

1740 Schneider, H. *Die Bedeutung der Geistestaufe in der charismatischen Erneuerung der Katholischen Kirche*. Wetzhausen, 1974.

1741 Schöpwinkel, Hermann. *Enthusiastisches Christentum oder Flugfeuer fremden Geistes?* Verlag der Liebenzeller Mission, 1970.

1742 Schreck, Alan Edward. "Ronald Knox's Theory of Enthusiasm and Its Application to the Catholic Charismatic Renewal." Unpublished doctor's dissertation, University of St. Michael's College, 1979.

1743 Schrenk, Elias. *Wir sahen Seine Herrlichkeit. Betrachtungen über das hohepriesterliche Gebet*. Ernst Röttger, 1896.

1744 Schulz, Siegfried. *Die Stunde der Botschaft. Einführung in die theologie der vier Evangelisten*. Furche-Verlag, 1967.

1745 Schütter, Günter. *Die letzten tibetischen Orakelpriester*. Franz, n.d.

1746 Schweizer, Eduard. *Church Order in the New Testament*. SCM Press, 1961.

1747 _____. "Was ist der Heilige Geist? Eine bibel-theologische Hinführung," *Concilium*, 15:10 (1979): 494-98.

1748 _____. "πνεῦμα, πνευματικός," in *Theological Dictionary of the New Testament*, Gerhard Kittel, editor. Trans. Geoffrey W. Bromiley. 10 vols. Eerdmans, 1964-1976. 6: 332-451.

1749 Scott, C. A. Anderson. "What Happened at Pentecost," in *The Spirit: The Relation of God and Man*, B. H. Streeter, editor. Macmillan and Company, 1919. Pp. 115-53.

1750 Scott, E. F. *The Spirit in the New Testament*. George H. Doran Company, 1923.

1751 Scott, John R. W. *The Baptism and Fullness of the Holy Spirit*. Inter-Varsity Press, 1964.

1752 Scottish Church Society. *The Pentecostal Gift*. Maclehose, 1903.

1753 Scroggie, W. Graham. *The Baptism of the Holy Spirit and Speaking with Tongues*. Marshall, Morgan and Scott, 1956.

1754 _____. *Speaking with Tongues*. Book Stall, 1919.

1755 Scroggs, Robin. "The Exaltation of the Spirit by Some Early Christians," *Journal of Biblical Literature*, 84 (1965): 359-73.

1756 Seamonds, David A. *Tongues: Psychic and Authentic—A Biblical Study of the Holy Spirit and the Gift of Tongues*. Privately published, 1972.

1757 Sebree, Herbert T. "Glossolalia," in *The Word and the Doctrine: Studies in Contemporary Wesleyan Arminian Theology*, Kenneth E. Geiger, editor. Logos International, 1965. Pp. 335-51.

1758 Secrétan, Louis. *Baptême des croyants ou baptême des enfants?* Editions du Grenie 20, 1946.

1759 Seddon, A. E. "Edward Irving and Unknown Tongues," *Homiletic Review*, 58 (1957): 103.

1760 Séguy, J. "Pentecôtisme," *Encyclopaedia Universalis*, 12 (1968): 754.

1761 _____. "La Protestation implicite: groupes et communautes charismatiques," *Archies de sciences sociales des religions*, 24 (October-December 1979): 187-212.

1762 Seitz, Johann and Ernst F. Ströter. *Die Selbstentlarvung von "Pfingst"-Geistern*. Montanus u. Ehrenstein, 1911.

1763 Shahinian, Dean. "The Jesus People," *The American Church*, 15:7 (1972): 10-15.

1764 Sharot, Stephen. "Hasidism and the Routinization of Charisma," *Journal for Scientific Study of Religion*, 19 (December 1980): 325-36.

1765 Sheppard, W. T. C. "The Gift of Tongues in the Early Church," *American Ecclesiastical Review*, 42 (January-June 1910): 513-22.

1766 Sherrill, John L. *They Speak with Other Tongues*. McGraw Hill, 1964.

1767 Short, Stephen N. "Pentecostal Student Movement at Howard: 1946-1977," *Spirit*, 1:2 (1977): 11-23.

1768 Shuler, R. P. *McPhersonism: A Study of Healing Cults and Modern Day Tongues Movements*. Privately published, 1924.

1769 Shumacher, W. R. "The Use of Ruah in the Old Testament and of Pneuma in the New Testament: A Lexicographical Study," *Journal of Biblical Literature*, 23 (1904): 13-67.

1770 Shumway, Charles William. "A Critical History of Glossolalia." Unpublished doctor's dissertation, Boston University, 1919.

1771 Siirala, Aarne. "A Methodological Proposal," in "Symposium on Speaking in Tongues," *Dialog*, 2 (1963): 158-59.

1772 Simmel, O. "Die Katholische Pfingstbewegung in den Vereinigten Staaten," *Internationale Katholische Zeitschrift*, 2 (1973): 148-57.

1773 Simmonds, Robert B., James T. Richardson and Mary W. Harder. "Jesus Movement Group: An Adjective Checklist Assessment," *Journal for the Scientific Study of Religion*, 15 (December 1976): 323-37.

1774 _____. "Organizational Aspects of a Jesus Movement Community," *Social Compass*, 21:3 (1974): 269-81.

1775 Simmons, E. L. *History of the Church of God*. Church of God Publishing House, 1938.

1776 Simmons, J. P. *History of Tongues*. Privately published, n.d.

1777 Simon, T. *Die Psychologie des Apostels Paulus*. N.p., 1897.

1778 Simpson, Albert B. *The Holy Spirit, or Power From on High*. Christian Alliance Publishing Company, 1924.

1779 Simpson, George Eaton. "Black Pentecostalism in the U.S.," *Phylon*, 35 (1974): 203-11.

1780 Sion, Etienne. "The Charismatic Nature of the Local Church," *African Ecclesiastical Review*, 18:3 (1976): 160-65.

1781 Sirks, G. J. "The Cinderella of Theology: The Doctrine of the Holy Spirit," *Harvard Theological Review*, 50 (April 1957): 77-89.

1782 Sirotko, Theodore Francis. *An Analysis of the Charismatic Movement Within the Episcopal Diocese of Hawaii*, San Francisco Theological Seminary, 1982.

1783 Skinner, B. F. *Verbal Behavior*. Appleton-Century-Crofts, 1957.

1784 Slay, James L. "Glossolalia: Its Value to the Individual," in *The Glossolalia Phenomenon*, Wade H. Horton, editor. Pathway Press, 1966. Pp. 217-43.

1785 Sleeper, Charles F. "Pentecost and Resurrection," *Journal of Biblical Literature*, 84 (December 1965): 389-99.

1786 Smail, Thomas. *Reflected Glory: The Spirit in Christ and Christians*. Hodder & Stoughton, 1975.

1787 Smalley, Stephen S. "Spiritual Gifts and 1 Corinthians 12-16," *Journal of Biblical Literature*, 88 (1968): 427-33.

1788 Smeeton, Donald D. "Holiness Hymns and Pentecostal Power: A Theologican Looks at Pentecostal Hymnody," *The Hymn*, 31 (July 1980): 183-85.

1789 _____. "A Pentecostal Looks Again at Vatican II," *Pneuma*, 5:1 (Spring 1983): 34-45.

1790 _____. "Perfection or Pentecost: A Historical Comparison of Charismatic and Holiness Theologies." Unpublished master's thesis, Trinity Evangelical Divinity School, 1971.

1791 Smet, Walter. *Ik Maak Alles Nieuw: Charismatische beweging in de kerk*. Privately published, 1973.

1792 Smith, Aaron A. *The Holy Spirit and His Workings*. Privately published, n.d.

1793 Smith, B. L. "Tongues in the New Testament," *Churchman*, 87 (Winter 1973): 283-88.

1794 Smith, Charles R. "Biblical Conclusions Concerning Tongues." Unpublished doctor's dissertation, Grace Theological Seminary, 1970.

1795 _____. *Tongues in Biblical Perspective*. BMH Books, 1972.

1796 Smith, D. Moody. "Glossolalia and Other Spiritual Gifts in a New Testament Perspective," *Interpretation*, 28 (July 1974): 307-20.

1797 Smith, Daniel Stephen. "Glossolalia: The Personality Correlates of Conventional and Unconventional Subgroups." Unpublished doctor's dissertation, Rosemead Graduate School of Professional Psychology, 1977.

1798 Smith, Frank W. "What Value Tongues?" *Message of the Open Bible*, 45 (June 1963): 4-5.

1799 Smith, Kenneth G. "The 'Mystery' of the Holy Spirit," *Blue Banner Faith and Life*, 19 (January-March 1964): 3-6.

1800 Smith, Miles W. *On Whom the Spirit Came*. The Judson Press, 1948.

1801 Smith, Swinburne. "Speaking with Tongues: The Gift and the Sign," *Pentecostal Evangel*, 44 (August 9, 1964): 7.

1802 Smith, Timothy L. *Called Unto Holiness: The Story of the Nazarenes: The Formative Years*. Nazarene Publishing House, 1962.

1803 _____. *Revivalism and Social Reform: American Protestantism on the Eve of the Civil War*. Harper and Row, 1965.

1804 _____. *Speaking the Truth in Love: Some Honest Questions for Pentecostals*. Beacon Hill Press, 1977.

1805 Smith, Wilbur M. "Notes on the Literature of Pentecostalism," *Moody Monthly*, 56 (December 1955): 33-37.

1806 Smolchuck, Fred. *Tongues and Total Surrender*. Gospel Publishing House, 1974.

1807 Smylie, James H. "Testing the Spirits in the American Context: Great Awakenings, Pentecostalism, and the Charismatic Movements," *Interpretation*, 33 (1979): 32-46.

1808 Sneck, William Joseph. *Charismatic Spiritual Gifts*. University Press of America, 1981.

1809 Snyder, Dean J. "Confessions of a Closet Charismatic," *Christian Century*, 100 (May 1983): 878-81.

1810 Snyder, Howard A. "The Church as Holy and Charismatic," *Wesley Theological Journal*, 15 (Fall 1980): 7-32.

1811 Snyder, Howard A. and Quincy Smith-Newcomb. "Servant Band: Prophets to the Rock Generation—the Jesus Movement Is Still Alive," *Christianity Today*, 26 (October 26, 1982): 76-77.

1812 Soltan, George. "The Tongues Movement," *Our Hope*, 55 (June 1949): 751-55.

1813 Sorem, Anthony M. "Some Secular Implications of the Pentecostal Denomination." Unpublished master's thesis, University of Minnesota, 1969.

1814 "Speaking in Tongues," *Time*, 76 (August 15, 1960): 53, 55.

1815 "Speaking with Other Tongues," *The Pentecostal Evangel*, (April 26, 1964): 9-11.

1816 Speer, Blanche C. "A Linguistic Analysis of a Corpus of Glossolalia." Unpublished doctor's dissertation, University of Colorado at Boulder, 1971.

1817 Spence, Hubert T. *Pentecost Is Not A Tangent*. Pentecostal Holiness Church, n.d.

1818 Spence, Othniel T. *Charismatism: Awakening or Apostasy?* Bob Jones University Press, 1978.

1819 Spittler, Russell. *Perspectives of New Pentecostalism*. Baker Book House, 1976.

1820 _____. "The Theological Opportunity Lying Before the Pentecostal Movement," in *Aspects of Pentecostal-Charismatic Origins*, Vinson Synan, editor. Logos International, 1975. Pp. 235-43.

1821 Spörri, T., ed. *Beiträge zur Ekstase*, (Bibliotheca Psychiatrica et Neurologica 135). S. Karger, 1968.

1822 Stagg, Frank. "Glossolalia in the New Testament," in *Glossolalia: Tongue Speaking in Biblical, Historical, and Psychological Perspective*, Frank Stagg, E. Glenn Hinson, and Wayne E. Oates, editors. Abingdon Press, 1967. Pp. 20-44.

1823 Stanley, Arthur P. "The Gift of Tongues and the Gift of Prophesying," in *A Collection of Theological Essays from Various Authors*, George R. Noyes, compiler. William Crosby, 1856. Pp. 453-71.

1824 Stanley, Gordon, et al. "Some Characteristics of Charismatic Experience: Glossolalia in Australia," *Journal for the Scientific Study of Religion*, 17 (Spring 1978): 269-77.

1825 Stark, Rodney. "Psychopathology and Religious Commitment," *Review of Religious Research*, 2 (1971): 165-76.

1826 "A Statement with Regard to Speaking in Tongues," *Reports and Actions of the Second General Convention of the American Lutheran Church*. The American Lutheran Church, 1964.

1827 Steadman, J. M. "Anent 'the Gift of Tongues' and Kindred Phenomena," *Methodist Quarterly Review*, 74 (October 1925): 688-715.

1828 Stegall, Carroll, Jr. *The Modern Tongues and Healing Movement*. Western Bible Institute, n.d.

1829 Steindl-Rast, David F. K. "Charismatic Renewal, A Challenge to Roman Catholic Worship," *Worship*, 48:7 (September 1974): 382-91.

1830 Steiner, Leonhard. *Le baptême de l'Esprit et l'appartenance au Corps de Christ, d'après 1 Cor. 12:13*. Basel, n.d.

1831 Steinmetz, David. "The Charismatic Movement and the New Testament," *What the Spirit is Saying to the Churches*, Theodore Runyon, editor. Hawthorne Books, 1975. Pp. 17-28.

1832 _____. "Glossolalia and the Charismatic Movement," *God's Christ and His People*, Jacob Jervell and Wayne A. Meeks, editors. Universitetsforlaget, 1977. Pp. 122-31.

1833 _____ "Religious Ecstasy in Staupitz and the Young Luther," *The Sixteenth Century Journal*, 11:1 (1980): 23-37.

1834 Stemme, Harry A. *Speaking with Other Tongues: Sign and Gift*. Northern Gospel Publishing House, 1946.

1835 Stendahl, Krister. "The New Pentecostalism: Reflections of an Ecumenical Observer," in *Perspectives on the New Pentecostalism*, Russell F. Spittler, editor. Baker Book House, 1976. Pp. 194-207.

1836 _____. "The New Testament Evidence," in *The Charismatic Movement*, Michael P. Hamilton, editor. Eerdmans, 1975. Pp. 49-60.

1837 Stephanou, Eusebius A. "Charismata in the Early Church Fathers," *Greek Orthodox Theological Review*, 21 (Summer 1976): 125-46.

1838 Stephens, Elizabeth C. "Goodbye, My Pentecost," *St. Luke's Journal of Theology*, 21 (December 1977): 49-59.

1839 Sterner, Russell Eugene. "Do All Speak in Tongues?" *Vital Christianity*, 94 (October 6, 1974): 15-17.

1840 Sterrett, T. Norton. "The New Testament Charismata." Unpublished doctor's dissertation, Dallas Theological Seminary, 1947.

1841 Stevenson, Ian. "Book Review of Morton T. Kelsey's *Tongue Speaking*," in *Journal of the American Society for Psychical Research*, 60 (1966): 300-303.

1842 _____. *Xenoglossy*. University Press of Virginia, 1974.

1843 Stevenson, Kenneth W. "The Catholic Apostolic Church: Its History and Its Eucharist," *Studia Liturgica*, 13:1 (1979): 21-45.

1844 Stibbs, A. M. "Putting the Gift of Tongues in its Place," *Churchman*, 80 (Winter 1966): 295-305.

1845 Stiles, John E. *The Gift of the Holy Spirit*. Privately published, n.d.

1846 ————. *How to Receive the Holy Spirit*. Revell, 1971.

1847 Stinnette, Charles R. "On the Nature of Gifts and Gift-Giving," *Journal of Pastoral Care*, 8 (Winter 1954): 218-22.

1848 Stokes, Mark Boyd. *The Holy Spirit and Christian Experience*. Graded Press, 1975.

1849 Stockmayer, Otto. *La maladie et l'Evangile*. Neuchâtel, 1878.

1850 Stolee, Haakon J. *Pentecostalism: The Problem of the Modern Tongues Movement*. Augsburg Publishing House, 1936.

1851 ————. *Speaking in Tongues*. Augsburg Publishing House, 1963.

1852 Stoll, R. F. "The First Christian Pentecost," *Ecclesiastical Review*, 108 (1943): 337-47.

1853 Stone, D. D. "The Speaking in Tongues and the Episcopal Church," *Trinity*, 1 (Eastertide 1962): 10.

1854 Stone, Jean. "California Episcopalians Receive Pentecostal Baptism," *Pentecostal Testimony*, 46 (June 1962): 8-9.

1855 ————. "What Is Happening Today in the Episcopal Church?" *Christian Life*, 32 (November 1961): 38-41.

1856 Stone, Jean and Harald Bredesen. *The Charismatic Renewal in the Historic Churches*. The Blessed Trinity Society, n.d.

1857 Stonehouse, N. B. "Repentance, Baptism, and the Gift of the Holy Spirit," *The Westminster Theological Journal*, 13 (November 1950): 1-18.

1858 Stones, Christopher. "Jesus People: Fundamentalism and Changes in Factors Associates with Conservatism," *Journal for the Scientific Study of Religion*, 17 (June 1978): 155-58.

1859 Storey, William. "Reform or Suppression: Alternatives Seen for Catholic Charismatic Renewal." Unpublished paper, Notre Dame University, 1975.

1860 Stort, John R. W. *The Baptism and Fullness of the Holy Spirit*. Inter-Varsity Press, 1971.

1861 Stotts, George R. "Pentecostal Archival Material: Its Nature and Availability with Emphasis on the Southwest." A paper presented at the American Academy of Religion, Southwest Region, Sherman, Texas, March 15, 1974.

1862 Stover, Gene. *He Shall Baptize You with the Holy Ghost*. Privately published, n.d.

1863 Stowe, C. "Tongues and the New Testament Church," *Christian Standard*, (July 25, 1976): 9.

1864 Strachan, Gordon. *The Pentecostal Theology of Edward Irving*. Darton, Longman and Todd, n.d.

1865 Stranger, Frank Bateman. *The Gifts of the Spirit*. Christian Publications, 1974.

1866 Strauss, Lehman. *Speaking in Tongues*. Bible Study Time, n.d.

1867 Streeter, B. H., ed. *The Spirit*. Macmillan and Company, 1919.

1868 Streiker, Lowell D. *The Jesus Trip: Advent of the Jesus Freaks*. Abingdon Press, 1971.

1869 Stringer, Randy C. *What the Bible Teaches About the Purpose of Tongue Speaking*. Privately published, 1971.

1870 Stronstad, Roger. "The Influence of the Old Testament on the Charismatic Theology of St. Luke," *Pneuma*, 2:1 (Spring 1980): 32-50.

1871 Struchen, Jeannette. *Zapped by Jesus*. J. B. Lippincott Co., 1972.

1872 Study Commission on Glossolalia, Episcopal Diocese of California, *Preliminary Report*, Division of Pastoral Services, 1963.

1873 Suenens, Léon Joseph. *Ecumenism and Charismatic Renewal: Theological and Pastoral Orientation*. Servant Books, 1978.

1874 _____. *A New Pentecost?* Translated by Francis Martin. The Seabury Press, 1973.

1875 Suenes, Léon Joseph and Camara Dom Helder. *Charismatic Renewal and Social Action: A Dialogue*. Darton, Longman & Todd, 1980.

1876 Sullivan, Francis A. " 'Baptism in the Holy Spirit': A Catholic Interpretation of the Pentecostal Experience," *Gregorianum*, 55 (1974): 49-66.

1877 _____. *Charisms and Charismatic Renewal: A Biblical and Theological Study*. Servant Books, 1982.

1878 _____. "The Ecclesiological Context of the Charismatic Renewal," in *The Holy Spirit and Power*, Kilian McDonnell, editor. Doubleday & Company, 1975. Pp. 119-38.

1879 _____. "The Pentecostal Movement," *Gregorianum*, 53 (1972): 237-66.

1880 _____. "Speaking in Tongues," *Lumen Vitae*, 31:2 (1976): 145-70.

1881 ——————. " 'Speaking in Tongues' in the New Testament and in the Modern Charismatic Renewal," in *The Spirit of God in Christian Life*, Edward Malatesta, editor. Paulist Press, 1977. Pp. 23-74.

1882 Sullivan, H. S. *The Interpersonal Theory of Psychiatry*. W. W. Norton, 1953.

1883 Summers, Ray. "Unknown Tongues: 1 Corinthians 14." Unpublished paper, Southern Baptist Theological Seminary, 1960.

1884 Swank, J. Grant. "A Plea to Some Who Speak in Tongues," *Christianity Today*, 19 (February 28, 1975): 12-13.

1885 Swanson, Guy E. "Trance and Possession: Studies of Charismatic Influence," *Review of Religious Research*, 19 (Spring 1978): 253-78.

1886 Swatos, William H. "The Disenchantment of Charisma: A Weberian Assessment of Revolution in a Rationalized World," *Sociological Analysis*, 42 (Summer 1981): 119-36.

1887 Sweet, J. P. N. "A Sign for Unbelievers: Paul's Attitude to Glossolalia," *New Testament Studies*, 13 (April 1967): 240-57.

1888 Swete, H. B. "Holy Spirit" in *A Dictionary of the Bible*, James Hastings, editor. 5 vols. Scribner's Sons, 1902. 2:402-11.

1889 ——————. *The Holy Spirit in the Ancient Church*. Macmillan and Company, 1912.

1890 ——————. *The Holy Spirit in the New Testament*. Macmillan and Company, 1910.

1891 Synan, H. Vinson, ed. *Aspects of Pentecostal Charismatic Origins*. Logos International, 1975.

1892 ——————. *Charismatic Bridges*. Word of Life, 1974.

1893 ——————. *The Holiness-Pentecostal Movement in the United States*. Eerdmans, 1971.

1894 ——————. *The Old-Time Religion: A History of the Pentecostal Holiness Church*. Advocate Press, 1973.

1895 ——————. "Pentecost in St. Peter's," *Christianity Today*, 19 (June 6, 1975): 45-46.

1896 ——————. "The Pentecostal Movement in the United States." Unpublished doctor's dissertation, University of Georgia, 1967.

T

1897 "Taming the Tongues," *Time*, 84 (July 10, 1964): 64-66.

1898 Tamkin, Warren E. " 'That Which is Perfect' 1 Corinthians 13:10." Unpublished paper, Grace Theological Seminary, 1949.

1899 Tan, Paul Lee. *The Interpretation of Prophecy*. BMH Books, 1974.

1900 Tappeiner, D. "The Function of Tongue Speaking for the Individual: A Psycho-Theological Model," *Journal of the American Scientific Affiliation*, (March 1974): 29.

1901 _____. "Psychological Paradigm for the Interpretation of the Charismatic Phenomenon of Prophecy," *Journal of Psychology and Theology*, 5 (Winter 1977): 23-29.

1902 Tavares, Levy. "A mensagem pentecostita e a realidade brasileira," *O Espírito Santo*, (1966): 33-36.

1903 Taylor, G. F. "Our Church History," *Pentecostal Holiness Advocate*, (January 20-April 21, 1921): 12-14.

1904 Taylor, James E. "A Perspective on Christian Glossolalia." Unpublished paper, 1975.

1905 Taylor, John V. *The Go-Between God: The Holy Spirit and the Christian Mission*. SCM Press, 1972.

1906 Taylor, R. O. P. "The Tongues at Pentecost," *Expository Times*, 40 (1928-29): 300-303.

1907 Taylor, Richard S. *Tongues: Their Purpose and Meaning*. Beacon Hill Press, 1973.

1908 Taylor, Vincent. "The Spirit in the New Testament," in *The Doctrine of the Holy Spirit*, Vincent Taylor, editor. Epworth Press, 1937. Pp. 39-68.

1909 Taylor, Willard H. "Baptism with the Holy Spirit: Promise of Grace or Judgement?" *Wesleyan Theological Journal*, 12 (Spring 1977): 16-25.

1910 Tennekes, Johannes. "Mouvement Pentecotiste Chilien et la Politique," *Social Compass*, 25:1 (1978): 55-80.

1911 Teuber, Andrew S. *Tongues of Fire*. Privately published, 1966.

1912 "Theological and Pastoral Orientations on the Catholic Charismatic Renewal." An unpublished paper presented at Milines, Belgium, May 21-26, 1974.

1913 Thibodeun, Philippe A. "A Study of the Catholic Pentecostal Movement in Ann Arbor." Unpublished report, Ann Arbor, n.d.

1914 Thieme, R. B. *Tongues*. Berachah Tapes and Publications, 1971.

1915 "The Third Force in Christendom," *Life*, 44 (June 9, 1958): 113-24.

1916 Thiselton, Anthony C. "The 'Interpretation' of Tongues: A New Suggestion in the Light of Greek Usage in Phils and Josephus," *Journal of Theological Studies*, 30:1 (1979): 15-36.

1917 Thoburn, J. M. *The Church of Pentecost*. Jennings and Graham, 1901.

1918 Thom, Robert. *The Holy Spirit and the Name*. N.p., n.d.

1919 Thomas, K. "Speaking in Tongues." Unpublished paper, Berlin Suicide Prevention Center, 1965.

1920 Thomas, Robert L. "The Holy Spirit and Tongues," *The King's Business*, 54 (May 1963): 9-11.

1921 _____. "Now Concerning Spiritual Gifts: A Study of 1 Corinthians 12-14." Unpublished notebook, 1974.

1922 _____. "Tongues Will Cease," *Journal of the Evangelical Theological Society*, 17:2 (1978): 81-89.

1923 Thomas, W. H. Griffith. *The Holy Spirit of God*. The Bible Institute Colportage Association, 1913.

1924 Thomson, James G. S. S. "Spiritual Gifts," in *Baker's Dictionary of Theology*, Everett Harrison, editor. Baker Book House, 1960. Pp. 497-500.

1925 Thomson, W. S. "Tongues at Pentecost: Acts 2," *Expository Times*, 38 (1926-27): 284-86.

1926 "Thousands of Charismatic Christians Celebrate Pentecost," *Christianity Today*, 26 (July 16, 1982): 34-35.

1927 Thrapp, Dan L. "Churches Look Closely at 'Gift of Tongues,' " *Los Angeles Times*, (March 17, 1963): H-6.

1928 Tidings, Judy. *Gathering a People: Catholic Saints in Charismatic Perspective*. Logos International, 1977.

1929 Tiede, David L. *Charismatic Figure as Miracle Worker*. Society of Biblical Literature Scholar's Press, 1972.

1930 Tinder, Donald G. "The Holy Spirit from Pentecost to the Present: Book Survey," *Christianity Today* 19 (May 19, 1975): 11-12, 16, 18, 20.

1931 Tinker, Frank A. "Strange Words that Threaten Protestant Unity," *Pageant*, 20 (June 1965): 80-85.

1932 Tinney, James S. "Black Origins of the Pentecostal Movement," *Christianity Today*, 16 (1971): 4-6.

1933 _____. "Black Pentecostals: Setting Up The Kingdom," *Christianity Today*, (December 5, 1975): 20, 42-43.

1934 _____. "The Blackness of Pentecostalism," *Spirit*, 3:2 (1979): 27-36.

1935 _____. "Exclusivist Tendencies in Pentecostal Self-Definition: A Critique from Black Theology," *Journal of Religious Thought*, 36 (Spring-Summer 1979): 32-49.

1936 _____. "The Right to Be Heard on Tongues," *Christianity Today*, 10 (September 16, 1966): 46-47.

1937 _____. "William J. Seymour (1855?-1920?): Father of Modern-Day Pentecostalism," *The Journal of the Interdenominational Theological Center*, 4 (Fall 1976): 34-44.

1938 Tinney, James S. and Stephen N. Shorts, eds. *In the Tradition of William J. Seymour*. Spirit Press, 1978.

1939 Tolbert, Malcolm. "The Place of Spiritual Gifts in Ministry," *The Theological Educator*, 14:1 (Fall 1983): 53-63.

1940 Tomlinson, Ambrose J. *Answering the Call of God*. White Wing Publishing House, n.d.

1941 _____. *God's Annointed Prophet of Wisdom: Choice Writings of A. J. Tomlinson in Times of His Greatest Anointings*. White Wing Publishing House, 1970.

1942 _____. *God's Twentieth Century Pioneer: A Compilation of Some of the Writings of A. J. Tomlinson*. White Wing Publishing House, 1962.

1943 _____. "Journal of Happenings: The Diary of A. J. Tomlinson, March 7, 1901-November 3, 1923." Files of the Church of God, n.d.

1944 "Tongues," in *Dictionary of the Bible*, John L. McKenzie, editor. Bruce Publishing Company, 1965. Pp. 896-97.

1945 "Tongues," in *The New Westminster Dictionary of the Bible*, Henry Snyder Gehman, editor. Westminster Press, 1970. P. 955.

1946 "Tongues, Gift of," in *A Dictionary of the Bible*, William Smith, editor. Revell, n.d. Pp. 714-16.

1947 "Tongues, Gift of," in *Encyclopedia Britannica*. 23 vols. William Benton, 1962. 22: 288-89.

1948 "Tongues, Gift of," in *An Encyclopedia of Religion*, Verilius Ferm, editor. The Philosophical Library, 1945. Pp. 789-90.

1949 "The Tongues Movement," *Independent*, 66 (June 10, 1909): 1286-89.

1950 "Tongues, Speaking and Writing in," in *Encyclopedia of Occultism*, Lewis Spence, editor. University Books, 1968. P. 414.

1951 Toon, Vita. "Charismatic Experience and Church Membership," *Churchman*, 90 (July-September 1976): 206-16.

1952 Torrey, Reuben A. *The Baptism with the Holy Spirit*. Revell, 1897.

1953 _____. *Is the Present "Tongues" Movement of God?* Bible Institute of Los Angeles, n.d.

1954 _____. *The Person and Work of the Holy Spirit*. Zondervan, n.d.

1955 _____. *The Person and Work of the Holy Spirit*. Revell, 1910.

1956 Toussaint, Stanley D. "First Corinthians Thirteen and the Tongues Question," *Bibliotheca Sacra*, 120 (October-December 1963): 311-16.

1957 Trigg, Joseph W. "The Charismatic Intellectual: Origen's Understanding of Religious Leadership," *Church History*, 50 (March 1981): 5-19.

1958 Trinity Society. *Why Tongues, Why Divisions?* The Blessed Trinity Society, n.d.

1959 Truland, Carl G. "The Confusion About Tongues," *Christianity Today*, 13 (December 6, 1968): 207-209.

1960 Truluck, Rembert. "A Study of the Relationships Between Hellenistic Religious Ecstasy and Corinthian Glossolalia." Unpublished seminar paper, Southern Baptist Theological Seminary, 1965.

1961 Tschiedel, Hans. "Ein Pfingstwunder im Apollonhymnos," *Zeitschrift für Religions—und Geistesgeschichte*, 27:1 (1975): 22-39.

1962 Tugwell, Simon. *Catholic Pentecostalism*. Catholic Truth Society, 1973.

1963 _____. *Did You Receive the Spirit?* Paulist Press, 1972.

1964 _____. "Le don des langues d'après le Nouveau Testament," *Vie Spirituelle*, 128 (January-February 1974): 49-62.

1965 _____. "The Gift of Tongues in the New Testament," *Expository Times*, 84 (February 1973): 137-40.

1966 _____. "Group Prayer and Contemplation," *New Blackfriars*, 52 (1971): 132-38.

1967 _____. "Reflections on the Pentecostal Doctrine of 'Baptism in the Holy Spirit,' " *The Heythrop Journal*, 13 (1972): 260-81, 402-14.

1968 Tugwell, Simon, George Every, John O. Mills, and Peter Hocken. *New Heaven, New Earth: An Encounter with Pentecostalism*. Darton, Longman and Todd, 1976.

1969 Turnbull, Grace H. *Tongues of Fire: A Bible of Sacred Scriptures of the Pagan World*. Macmillan and Company, 1929.

1970 Turnbull, Thomas Napier. *What God Hath Wrought: A Short History of the Apostolic Church*. Puritan Press, 1959.

1971 Turner, F. C. "Protestantism and Politics in Chile and Brazil," *Comparative Studies in Society and History*, 12 (1970): 13-29.

1972 Turner, William H. *Pentecost and Tongues*. Modern Publishing House, 1968.

1973 _____. *The Sanctified Way of Life*. Publishing House of the Pentecostal Holiness Church, 1948.

1974 _____. *Two Thousand Years of Pentecost*. Publishing House of the Pentecostal Holiness Church, 1947.

1975 Turrano, L. "El bautismo *in Spiritu Sancto et igni*," *Estudios Eclesiásticos*, 34 (1960): 807-17.

UV

1976 Underwood, Bernard E. *The Gifts of the Spirit: Supernatural Equipment for Christian Service*. Advocate Press, 1967.

1977 Unger, Merrill F. *The Baptism and Gifts of the Holy Spirit*. Moody Press, 1974.

1978 _____. *The Baptizing Work of the Holy Spirit*. Dunham Publishing Company, 1962.

1979 _____. *New Testament Teaching on Tongues*. Kregel Publications, 1971.

1980 _____. "The Significance of Pentecost," *Bibliotheca Sacra*, 122 (April-June 1965): 169-77.

1981 Urch, Walter H. *The Place of Spiritual Gifts in Pentecostal Churches*. Elim Publishing Company, 1955.

1982 Van Der Arendt, Gerrit. "Conformation and Charismatic Renewal," *African Ecclesiastical Review*, 20 (December 1978): 276-81.

1983 Van Dusen, Henry P. "Third Force in Christianity," *Life*, 50 (June 9, 1958): 113-24.

1984 Van Elderen, Bastiaan. "Glossolalia in the New Testament," *Bulletin of the Evangelical Theological Society*, 7 (Spring 1964): 53-58.

1985 VanSlyke, L. B. "Gift of Tongues," *McClure*, 38 (March 1912): 546-57.

1986 Versteeg, John M. *Perpetuating Pentecost*. Willet, Clark and Colby, 1930.

1987 Vidales, Raul. "Charisms and Political Action," in *Charisms in the Church*, Christian Duquoc and Casiano Floristan, editors. The Seabury Press, 1978. Pp. 67-77.

1988 Vié, Sr. E. "Le renouveau charismatique," *Christus*, 80 (October 1973): 497.

1989 *View: A Quarterly Journal Interpreting the World-Wide Charismatic Renewal*. Full Gospel Business Men's Fellowship International.

1990 Vigevend, H. S. *Jesus the Revolutionary*. Regal Books, 1971

1991 Vinson, Synan. *Aspects of Pentecostal-Charismatic Origins*. Logos International, 1975.

1992 Vivier, Lincoln Morse. "Glossolalia." Unpublished doctor's dissertation, University of Witwatersrand, 1960.

1993 _____. "Glossolalia in the New Testament," *Bulletin of the Evangelical Theological Society*, 7 (Spring 1964): 53-58.

1994 _____. "The Glossolalic and His Personality," in *Beiträge zur Ekstase*, T. Spörri, editor. S. Karger, 1968.

1995 Volz, Paul. *Der Geist Gottes und die verwandten Erscheinungen im Alten Testament und im anschliessenden Judentum*. J. C. B. Mohr, 1910.

1996 _____. "Pharisäer," *Die Religion in Geschichte und Gegenwart*, 4 (1930): 1178f.

WXYZ

1997 Wagner, C. P. "What About Tongues Speaking?" *Eternity*, 19 (March 1968): 24-26.

1998 Wagner, Peter. *Look Out! The Pentecostals Are Coming*. Creation House, 1974.

1999 Wald, Oletta. "The Challenge of the Jesus People," *Encounter*, 7:1/2 (1973): 2-3.

2000 Waldegrave, Charles. "Social and Personality Correlates of Pentecostalism: A Review of the Literature and a Comparison of Pentecostal Christian Students with Non-Pentecostal Christian Students." Unpublished doctor's dissertation, University of Waikato, 1972.

2001 Waldvogel, Edith L. "The 'Overcoming' Life: A Study in the Reformed Evangelical Contribution to Pentecostalism," *Pneuma*, 1:1 (Spring 1979): 7-19.

2002 _____. "The 'Overcoming Life': A Study in the Reformed Evangelical Origins of Pentecostalism" *Harvard Theological Review*, 71 (January-April 1978): 167-68.

2003 Walker, Dawson. *The Gift of Tongues and Other Essays*. T. & T. Clark, 1906.

2004 Walker, Paul L. "Charismatic Development in the Contemporary Church." Unpublished sermon, Hemphill Church of God, n.d.

2005 Wallis, Gerhard. "Jerusalem und Samaria als Koenigsstaedte: Auseinandersetzung mit einer these albrecht alts," *Vetas Testamentum*, 26 (October 1976): 480-96.

2006 Wallis, Roy. "The Social Construction of Charisma," *Social Compass*, 29:1 (1982): 25-39.

2007 Walsh, Vincent M. "Catholic Pentecostalism: A Bibliography," *Catholic Library World*, 53 (May-June 1982): 428-29.

2008 _____. *A Key to Charismatic Renewal in the Catholic Church*. Abbey Press, 1974.

2009 Walters, Stanley D. "Speaking in Tongues," *Youth in Action*, (May 1964): 8-11, 28.

2010 Walvoord, John F. "Contemporary Issues in the Doctrine of the Holy Spirit, Part IV: Spiritual Gifts Today," *Bibliotheca Sacra*, 130 (1973): 315-28.

2011 _____. *The Holy Spirit*. Dunham Publishing Company, 1958.

2012 _____. *The Holy Spirit: A Comprehensive Study of the Person and Work of the Holy Spirit*. Van Kampen Press, 1954.

2013 _____. *The Holy Spirit at Work Today*. Moody Press, 1973.

2014 Wamble, Hugh. "Glossolalia in Christian History," in *Tongues*, Luther B. Dyer, editor. LeRoi Publishers, 1971. Pp. 24-59.

2015 Wansborough, Henry. "Speaking in Tongues," *The Way*, 14:3 (July 1974): 193-201.

2016 Warburton, T. Rennie. "Holiness Religion: An Anomaly of Sectarian Typologies," *Journal for the Scientific Study of Religion*, 8 (1969): 130-39.

2017 Ward, Horace, S., Jr. "The Anti-Pentecostal Argument," in *Aspects of Pentecostal-Charismatic Origins*, Vinson Synan, editor. Logos International, 1975. Pp. 99-122.

2018 Ward, Wayne E. "The Significance of Glossolalia for the Church," in *Speaking in Tongues: Let's Talk about It*, Watson E. Mills, editor. Word Books, 1973. Pp. 143-51.

2019 _____. "Various Views of Tongue Speaking," in *Tongues*, Luther B. Dyer, editor. LeRoi Publishers, 1971. Pp. 9-23.

2020 Watkins-Jones, H. *The Holy Spirit in the Medieval Church*. Macmillan and Co., 1922.

2021 Watson, David. *I Believe in the Church*. Hodder & Stoughton and Eerdmans, 1978.

2022 Wead, Douglas. *Catholic Charismatics*. Creation House, 1974.

2023 Weaver, Gilbert B. " 'Tongues Shall Cease': 1 Corinthians 13:8." Unpublished research paper, Grace Theological Seminary, 1964.

2024 Webber, Robert and Donald Bloesch, eds. *The Orthodox Evangelicals: Who They Are and What They are Saying*. Thomas Nelson, 1978.

2025 Weber, Karl. "Katholische Pfingstbewegung in Amerika," Orientierung, 36 (1972): 84-86.

2026 Weber, Max. "The Nature of Charismatic Domination," in *Weber: Selections in Translation*, W. G. Runciman, editor. Cambridge University Press, 1978. Pp. 226-50.

2027 Weber, Wilfried. "Charismatische Bewegung und Theologie der Befreiung," *Zeitschrift für Missionwissenschft und Relegionswissenschaft*, 62 (January 1978): 40-45.

2028 Webster, Douglas. *Pentecostalism and Speaking with Tongues*. Highway Press, 1964.

2029 _____. "The Pentecostals," *Churchman*, 86 (Winter 1972): 290-92.

2030 Wedderburn, A. J. M. "Romans 8:26—Towards a Theology of Glossolalia?" *Scottish Journal of Theology*, 28:4 (1975): 369-77.

2031 Weinel, Heinrich. *Die Wirkungen des Geistes und Geister im nachapostolischen Zeitalter bis auf Irenäus*. J. C. B. Mohr, 1899.

2032 Weisman, Z. "Charismatic Leaders in the Era of the Judges," *Zeitschrift fuer die alttestamentliche Wissenschaft*, 89:3 (1977): 399-411.

2033 Weitbrecht, H. J. "Ekstatische Zunstände bei Schizophrenen," in *Beiträge zur Ekstase*, T. Spörri, editor. S. Karger, 1968.

2034 Welliver, Kenneth Bruce. "Pentecost and the Early Church." Unpublished doctor's dissertation, Yale University, 1961.

2035 Welmers, William E. "Glossolalia," *Christianity Today*, 7 (November 8, 1963): 19-20.

2036 Wesseln, Hermann. "Die Jesus People—neues religiöses Erwachen oder Umstieg auf die neue Droge Religion als Opium fürs Volk?" *Katechetische Blätter*, 97 (1972): 280-91.

2037 Westgarth, J. W. *The Holy Spirit and the Primitive Mind*. Victory Press, 1946.

2038 Westwood, Tom. "Speaking in Unknown Tongues," *Bible Treasury Notes*, 7 (May 1949): 3-5.

2039 Whalley, W. E. "Pentecostal Theology," *The Baptist Quarterly*, 27 (July 1978): 282-89.

2040 White, Alma B. *Demons and Tongues*. Pillar of Fire Publishers, 1936.

2041 White, T. A. *Pentecostal Catholics*. A.C.T.S. Publications, 1973.

2042 Whiting, Albert N. "The United House of Prayer for All People: A Case Study of a Charismatic Sect." Unpublished doctor's dissertation, The American University, 1952.

2043 Whitley, O. R. "When You Speak in Tongues: Some Reflections on the Contemporary Search for Ecstasy," *Encounter*, 35 (Spring 1974): 81-94.

2044 Whitney, J. "The Charismatic Renewal: What Is It All About?" Unpublished paper, Communication Center at Notre Dame, March 1974.

2045 Wieseler. "Über das glōssais lalein," *Theologische Studien und Kritiken*, 2 (1838): 703-72.

2046 Wilberger, Hans. *Biblische Welt*. Silva-Verlag, n.d.

2047 Wild, Robert. " 'It Is Clear That There Are Serious Differences Differences Among You' (1 Corinthians 1:11): The Charismatic Renewal Entering Religious Communities," *Review for Religious*, 32 (September 1973): 1093-1102.

2048 _____. "The Post-Charismatic Phenomena: A Theological Interpretation," *Review for Religions*, 41 (March-April 1982): 257-65.

2049 Wilkens, W. "Wassertaufe und Geistesempfang bei Lukas," *Theologische Zeitschrift*, 23 (1967): 26-47.

2050 Willems, Emilio. "Validation of Authority in Pentecostal Sects of Chile and Brazil," *Journal for the Scientific Study of Religion*, 6 (1967): 253-58.

2051 Willet, H. L. "Question Box: New Testament References to Glossolalia or Speaking in Other Tongues," *Christian Century*, 54 (March 24, 1937): 389.

2052 Williams, Cyril G. "Ecstaticism in Hebrew Prophecy and Christian Glossolalia," *Studies in Religion*, 3:4 (1973-1974): 320-38.

2053 _____. "Glossolalia as a Religious Phenomenon: 'Tongues' at Corinth and Pentecost," *Religion*, 5:1 (1975): 16-32.

2054 _____. *Tongues of the Spirit: A Study of Pentecostal Glossolalia and Related Phenomena*. University of Wales Press, 1981.

2055 Williams, George H. and Edith Waldvogel. "A History of Speaking in Tongues and Related Gifts," in *The Charismatic Movement*, Michael Hamilton, editor. Eerdmans, 1975. Pp. 61-113.

2056 Williams, Jerry Douglas. "The Modern Pentecostal Movement in America: A Brief Sketch of Its History and Thought," *Lexington Theological Quarterly*, 9:2 (April 1974): 50-60.

2057 Williams, J. Rodman. *The Era of the Spirit*. Logos International, 1971.

2058 _____. *The Gift of the Holy Spirit*. Logos International, 1977.

2059 _____. "Opinion," *Logos Journal*, 7:3 (May-June 1977): 35.

2060 _____. *The Pentecostal Reality*. Logos International, 1972.

2061 _____. "Pentecostal Theology: A Neo-Pentecostal Viewpoint," in *Perspectives on the New Pentecostalism*, Russell F. Spittler, editor. Baker Book House, 1976. Pp. 76-85.

2062 _____. "Profile of the Charismatic Movement," *Christianity Today*, 19 (February 28, 1975): 9-13.

2063 _____. "The Upsurge of Pentecostalism: Some Presbyterian/Reformed Comment," *The Reformed World*, 31 (1971): 339-48.

2064 Williams, Melvin D. *Community in a Black Pentecostal Church: An Anthropological Study*. University of Pittsburgh Press, 1974.

2065 _____. "Considerations of a Black Anthropologist Researching Pentecostalism," *Spirit*, 3:2 (1979): 20-26.

2066 Williams, Michael A. "The Life of Antony and the Domestication of Charismatic Wisdom," *Joural of the American Academy of Religion*, 48:3/4 (1982): 23-45

2067 Willis, Lewis J. "Glossolalia in Perspective," in *The Glossolalia Phenomenon*, Wade H. Horton, editor. Pathway Press, 1966. Pp. 247-84.

2068 Wilson, Bryan R. "The Pentecostalist Minister: Role Conflicts and Status Contradiction," *American Journal of Sociology*, 64 (1959): 494-504.

2069 Wilson, Everett A. "Sanguine Saints: Pentecostalism in El Salvador," *Church History*, 52 (June 1983): 186-98.

2070 Wilson, John and Harvey K. Clow. "Themes of Power and Control in a Pentecostal Assembly," *Journal for the Scientific Study of Religion*, 20 (September 1981): 241-50.

2071 Winehouse, Irwin. *The Assemblies of God: A Popular Survey*. Vantage Press, 1959.

2072 Winn, Albert C. "Holy Spirit and the Christian Life," *Interpretation*, 33 (January 1979): 47-57.

2073 Wirt, Sherwood Eliot. *Jesus Power*. Harper and Row, 1972.

2074 Wolfram, Walter Andrew. "The Sociolinguistics of Glossolalia." Unpublished master's thesis, Hartford Seminary, 1966.

2075　Womack, David A. *The Wellsprings of the Pentecostal Movement.* Gospel Publishing House, 1968.

2076　Wood, Laurence W. "Exegetical-Theological Reflections on the Baptism with the Holy Spirit," *Wesleyan Theological Journal*, 14 (Fall 1979): 51-63.

2077　_____. *Pentecostal Grace.* Asbury Publishing Co., 1980.

2078　Wood, William W. "Culture and Personality Aspects of the Pentecostal Holiness Religion." Unpublished doctor's dissertation, University of North Carolina, 1961.

2079　_____. *Culture and Personality Aspects of the Pentecostal Holiness Religion.* Mouton and Company, 1965.

2080　Woodrow, A. "Le Renouveau charismatique aux États-Unis," *Informations catholiques internationales*, 448 (January 15, 1974): 13-20. Cf. Nos. 437-38 (August 1973): 3-5.

2081　Woodside, Edmund R. "Glossolalia, the Gift of Tongues: A Bibliography," *Fuller Library Bulletin*, 11 (July-September 1951): 3-5.

2082　Woolsey, Warren. "Speaking in Tongues: A Biblical, Theological and Practical Study." Unpublished paper, Houghton, NY. Houghton Wesleyan Church, 1971.

2083　World Council of Churches. "Die Bedeutung der charismatischen Erneuerung für die Kirchen. Bericht einer Konsultation in Bossey," *Una Sancta*, 36:1 (1981): 5-10.

2084　_____. "Towards a Church Renewed and United in the Spirit," *The Ecumenical Review*, 31:3 (1979): 305-309.

2085　Wormus, J. W. "Jesus Movement," *Risk*, 11:4 (1975): 35-39.

2086　Worship: Blue Tongues," *Time*, 81 (March 29, 1963): 52.

2087　Worsley, Peter. *The Trumpet Shall Sound.* Macgibbon and Kee, 1957.

2088　Wotherspoon, Henry J. *What Happened at Pentecost.* T. & T. Clark, 1937.

2089　Wright, Arthur. "The Gift of Tongues: A New View," *Theological Monthly*, 5 (1891): 161-69, 272-80.

2090　Yi, Richard. "Spirit Baptism and Tongues in Acts." Unpublished bachelor's thesis, Talbot Theological Seminary, 1969.

2091　Yuasa, Key. "O Pentecostismo e as Igrejas protestantes," in ASTE, *O Espírito Santo*, (1966): 68-70.

2092 Zaleski, A. M. *Report to the United States Catholic Bishops* meeting in Washington, D.C., November 1969. Published in *Theology Digest*, 19 (1971): 52-53.

2093 Zaugg, E. A. *A Genetic Study of the Spirit Phenomena in the New Testament*. University of Chicago Press, 1917.

2094 Zeller, George W. *God's Gift of Tongues: The Nature, Purpose, and Duration of Tongues as Taught in the Bible*. Loizeaux Brothers, 1978.

2095 Zens, Jon. "An Appraisal of the Charismatic Movement," *Baptist Reformation Review*, 11:2 (1982): 43-47.

2096 Zimmerman, Charles. "The Gift of Tongues in 1 Corinthians." Unpublished paper, Grace Theological Seminary, n.d.

2097 Zimmerman, Thomas F. "The Pentecostal Position," *The Pentecostal Evangel*, (February 10, 1963): 2-3, 7.

2098 _____. "Plea for the Pentecostalists," *Christianity Today*, 7 (January 4, 1963): 11-12.

2099 _____. "Priorities and Beliefs of Pentecostals," *Christianity Today*, 25 (September 4, 1981): 36-67.

2100 _____. "Rags to Riches," *Christian Life*, 28 (July 1966): 32-33, 55-56.

2101 _____. "The Reason for the Rise of the Pentecostal Movement," in *Aspects of Pentecostal-Charismatic Origins*, Vinson Synan, editor. Logos International, 1975. Pp. 5-13.

2102 _____. "Where Is the 'Third Force' Going?" *Christianity Today*, 4 (August 1, 1960): 15-16, 18.

2103 Zohiates, Spiros. *Speaking with Tongues*. American Mission to Greeks, 1964.

2104 _____. *What the Bible Says about Tongues*. American Mission to the Greeks, 1964.

2105 Zylberberg, Jacques and Jean Montminy. "Reproduction socio-politique et Production symbolique: engagement et désengagement des charismatiques catholiques québécois," *The Annual Review of the Social Sciences of Religions*, 4 (1980): 121-48.

INDEXES

[These indexes contain references to page numbers in the introduction (set in roman type) and references to the numbered bibliographical entries (set in bold type). In every case the former citations will consist of either one or two integers while the latter will consist of three or four.]

Editors and Joint Authors

Lynd, Helen Merrell. **1209**.

McDonnell, Kilian. 5, 12, **181**, **1298**, **1878**.

McKenzie, John L. **1944**.

McTernan, John. **1319**.

Mäki, Pertti. **196**.

Malatesta, Edward. **1881**.

Malony, Newton. **1202**.

Martin, Francis. **1874**.

Martin, Ira J. 4.

Martin, Marty. 4.

Martin, Ralph. **1588**.

Martoch, E. J. **864**.

Meeks, Wayne A. **1832**.

Melton, John Gordon. 11.

Meyer, H. **900**.

Meyer, R. **1236**.

Michael, R. **405**.

Middleton, J. **109**.

Mills, John O. **1968**.

Mills, Watson E. 4, 14, **280**, **841**, **876**, **1229**, **1316**, **1408**, **1498**, **1705**, **2018**.

Moltman, Jürgen. **222**, **646**.

Montminy, Jean. **2105**.

Moore, Everett L. 7.

Moore, Ruth K. **307**.

Morisy, Ann. **829**.

Mühlen, Heribert. 5, **163**, **840**.

Murray, Andrew. 15.

Nelson, P. C. 15, **666**.

Newman, Richard. **285**.

Nichol, John Thomas. 4.

Noyes, George R. **1823**.

Oates, Wayne E. **873**, **1438**, **1822**.

O'Connell, Daniel. **274**.

O'Connor, Edward D. 11, 12, **227**, **1135**, **1446**, **1447**.

Olila, James H. **872**.

Opsahl, Paul D. **633**.

Osborne, Grant R. **1545**.

Ove, Hanssen. **540**.

Parham, Charles Fox. 7.

Parham, Sarah E. 7.

Paton, John I. **545**.

Pattison, E. Mansell. **1502**.

Pearlman, Myer. 15, **666**.

Pederson, Duane. 13.

Peters, C. Breckenridge. **542**.

Pettay, L. **224**.

Phypers, David. **255**.

Pickering, H. **676**.

Prince, Raymond. **226**.

Qualben, Paul. **1077**.

Ramsey, James W. **1283**.

Ranaghan, Dorothy. 11, **1593**.

Ranaghan, Kevin. 11.

Reidy, M. T. V. **1630**.

Remy, Jean. **853**.

Richardson, James T. 13, **1773**.

Roberts, J. D. **647**.

Roberts, Oral. 8, 9, 10.

Rops, Daniel. **643**.

Runciman, W. G. **2026**.

Runyon, Theodore. **485**, **1831**.

Schneck, Jerome M. **1318**.

Seymour, William J. 7.

Shakarian, Demos. 9.

Shepherd, Gerald T. **071**.

Sherill, John L. 5.

Shorts, Stephen N. **1938**.

Simmons, E. L. 8.

Simon, Pierre-Henry. **643**.

Simpson, John H. **1136**.

Sirks, G. J. 1.

Smith, William. **1946**.

Smith-Newcomb, Quincy. **1811**.

Spence, Lewis. **1950**.

Spittler, Russell F. 12, **058**, **282**, **534**, **568**, **606**, **649**, **681**, **927**, **961**, **1060**, **1228**, **1237**, **1542**, **1710**, **1835**, **2061**.

Spörri, T. **1994**, **2033**.

Stagg, Frank. 13, **873**, **1438**, **1822**.

Starkes, M. Thomas. **1355**.

Stone, Jean. 11.

Streeter, B. H. **1749**.

Ströter, Ernst F. **1762**.

Subject